# A Class Apart

*The Gentry Families of*
*County Kildare*

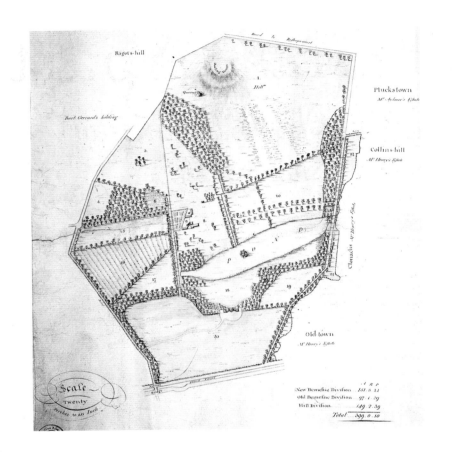

Bagot's-hill

Road to Rathangrourt

Pluckstown
Mr Aylmer's Estate

Hill.

Quarry

Bart Gerrard's holding

Collins-hill
Mr Henry's Estate

Clonalis Mr Henry's Estate

Old town
Mr Henry's Estate

Scale
Twenty
Perches to an Inch

|  | A R P |
|---|---|
| New Demesne Division | 151 3 22 |
| Old Demesne Division | 97 1 29 |
| Hill Division | 149 2 39 |
| Total | 399 0 10 |

# A Class Apart

## The Gentry Families of County Kildare

Con Costello

NONSUCH

*Frontispiece:* A map of the demesme of Lyons, surveyed by John Roe, 1796 (National Library of Ireland). Originally the seat of the Alymers, the estate was sold in that year to Nicholas Lawless, the first Lord Cloncurry, who built Lyons House in 1797.

First published 2005

Nonsuch Publishing
73 Lower Leeson Street
Dublin 2
Ireland
www.nonsuchireland.com

National Library Cataloguing in Publication Data.
A catalogue record for this book is available from the National Library.

ISBN 1 84588 504 X

Typesetting and origination by Tempus Publishing Limited.
Printed in Great Britain.

# Contents

# Acknowledgements

Sincere appreciation is due to the many people who assisted in my research for this material: Mary Clements, Caroline de Robeck, John de Burgh, and the late Maud Wolfe; Mario Corrigan, Kildare Local History Librarian; Elizabeth Gleeson, Law Librarian, TCD; Ray Gillespie, NUI, Maynooth; the staff of the National Gallery and the National Library. Also appreciation to Noelle Moran, editor at Nonsuch Publishing, for her encouragement; to Anne Fitzsimons for her helpful comments, my sons Denis and Con for practical support, and especially to Maeve for her patience and sustenance.

Tullig, Naas.
1 September 2005.

# The Author

For over twenty years Con Costello has entertained Leinster Leader readers with weekly stories from Kildare County's history. His many other books include; *A Most Delightful Station: British Army on the Curragh of Kildare, Kildare: Saints, Soldiers and Horses* and *Botany Bay, the Story of the Convicts transported to Australia*. He is Chairman of Kildare County Council Monuments Committee, a former Heritage Council member and former President of the Kildare Archaeological Society.

# Colour Illustrations

# Black & White Illustrations

# Foreword

Ireland in the twentieth century has had an ambiguous relationship with its gentry. On the one hand they were a reminder of the stereotypical oppressive, rack-renting landlord of the nineteenth century, a view much favoured and endorsed in newly independent Ireland as the Land Commission continued the process of breaking up the older estates. On the other hand they resembled the lovable and gullible Major Yeates of the nostalgic world of the Irish RM evoked by Somerville and Ross. Similarly the world of the 'big house' has drawn forth contrasting responses, some seeing those buildings as the symbol of privilege and ascendancy while others regarded them as part of the nation's cultural history with an eye to their tourist potential as attractive places to visit or to establish a golf or country club for the new Irish gentry. In the early twenty-first century those attitudes are beginning to shift. The nineteenth-century attitudes of hierarchy and deference that survived into the 1970s are changing rapidly. As a result the world of the landlord is losing its political meaning and beginning to fall into the category of the 'foreign country' that historians investigate.

Recent work on Irish landlords in the nineteenth century has demonstrated the diversity of that community. Boundaries created by older perceptions have come to be blurred by further investigation. The nineteenth-century champion of the tenant, Fr Patrick Lavelle, author of the *The Irish Landlord since the Revolution*, was on visiting and dining terms with the one of the great Connacht landlords, Lord Ardilaun. There were those who lived up to the image of Lord Leitrim but equally there were those who did much to improve the lot of their tenants, often at the cost of bankruptcy after the bad years of the Famine. As Con Costello reminds us 'If the crimes of the bad landlords are remembered, the humanity and benevolence of others are often forgotten'.

There is perhaps no better place in Ireland to investigate the world of the gentry than County Kildare. As this book demonstrates, the gentry of Kildare were an eclectic mix. From one of Ireland's socially most powerful families, the dukes of Leinster to the lesser Alymers, Wogans and Eustaces this group contained a great diversity of origins, wealth, and social attitudes while all being part of 'a class apart'. Moreover almost none of them conform to the popular images of the Irish gentry in the eighteenth and nineteenth centuries. The O'More-Ferrall's were of Irish origin despite the perception that the gentry were colonists. Others, such as the Aylmers, Browns, Wogans and Mansfields were Catholic and yet most observers understand the terms 'gentry' and 'Protestantism' to be coterminous. Moreover, in the area of political activity Con Costello's comment on the Aylmers that 'men of the family fought on both the government and rebel sides' in 1798 could be applied to many of the Kildare families.

This book extracts the gentry from the political debates of twentieth-century Ireland and restores them to their own world with its unique contradictions and complexities. By focusing on all the gentry of Kildare a complex array of characters appear in sharp focus. Some were remarkable men, although few would now recognise their names. In the nineteenth century the duke of Leinster was one of those who promoted the study of Irish antiquities and his son Lord Walter was one of the prime movers in establishing on a firm footing the Kildare Archaeological Society, now the oldest local history society in Ireland, and contributing an incredible number of papers to its journal. All this he did while running an estate and acting as a trustee of the duke's estate as it was being sold. He was truly 'an exceptional gentleman'. Also involved as a founder in that early society was the seventh earl of Mayo but, as Con Costello reveals, his family's involvement with promoting and advancing local communities did not end there. Mayo's father was viceroy of India and the seventh earl was actively involved in local politics. In 1922 he became a senator in the Free State. His wife was also involved with local society, encouraging local industry and craft working.

Lord Walter and the earl of Mayo are just two of the lesser-known but fascinating characters that you will encounter in this book. Con Costello has brought his unique knowledge of the evidence for the recreation of a world that has gone and an understanding of the problems and challenges that the inhabitants of that world faced to portray, in all its diversity, a society that still continues to shape our own world. The result is a book that expands our own vista.

Dr Raymond Gillespie
*NUI Maynooth*

# 1

# The Golden Years

In medieval times Ireland was ruled by an aristocratic hierarchy of regional kings, known as *rí tuaithe,* but following the Anglo-Norman invasion of the twelfth century the structure of society began to change drastically. The ancient Gaelic territories were divided into counties, gradually a new aristocracy evolved, and in County Kildare the dominant FitzGerald dynasty was to survive for almost eight hundred years. Succeeding centuries brought even more unwelcome adventurers, especially following the upheavals of the sixteenth century Reformation. The later successful campaign of Oliver Cromwell, followed by land confiscations subsequent to the victory of King William at Aughrim on the fateful 12 July 1691, and the introduction of penal laws against Catholics, were to alter indelibly the structure of Irish society.

In Kildare, the coincidence of the Reformation with the decline of the lordly FitzGerald family, following the revolt of Silken Thomas and his execution with that of his five uncles in London in February 1537, had enabled the emergence of a new dominant order.

Benefiting from the redistribution of confiscated monastic lands and houses, and the sequestered estates of the earl of Kildare and his supporters, were the families of Eustace, Sutton, Aylmer, Bermingham, Wellesley and Colley, as well as recently arrived English officials such the Alens. A century later Dean Swift, at a time when the Irish people were commonly referred to in the Dublin Parliament as 'the domestic enemy,' characterized the Irish (Protestant) squire of his day: 'almost to a man an oppressor of the clergy, a racker of his tenants, a jobber of all public works, and generally illiterate.'

While the majority of the Kildare gentry were of Anglo-Norman ancestry and long resident in Ireland, others were descended from grantees of the Elizabethan and Cromwellian eras, or later arrivals from England. But there were a few obvious exceptions: the ancestor of the Conollys of Castletown was an Irish innkeeper who had conformed to the Established Church, the La Touches of Harristown were of Huguenot background and the first de Robeck had come to Ireland from Sweden.

A list of the *County Kildare Gentry* in 1600 included forty-seven families, but only six of those families survived to be named amongst the thirty-five *Gentlemen of County Kildare* recorded in 1772. The new gentry, who replaced those who had acquired land in the catastrophic sixteenth and seventeenth centuries, were sometimes wealthy Dublin businessmen who sought to become gentlemen by purchasing or building country houses adjacent to the capital. Some of the gentry, who were supportive of the making of the Grand Canal through the county in the eighteenth century, were given permanent memorials when specific structures were named after them: the *Leinster Aqueduct* over the Liffey and *Duke's Harbour* at Maynooth confirmed the Duke of Leinster's involvement in the scheme, while bridges were named after others, including Burgh, Digby, Ponsonby, Aylmer and Henry.

*Hunt protest at
Moore Abbey,
Kildare, 1887
The tensions
between gentry and
common people
are depicted in the
Illustrated London
News.
The original
caption is: The
State of Ireland:
Farmers stopping
the Reloare hunt
at the Marquis of
Drogheda's Gate,
in Kildare*

In the last decades of the eighteenth century five families in the county had received new titles. The Stratfords were created Earls of Aldborough, the Bourkes of Palmerstown received the title Earl of Mayo, and John Scott was advanced to the dignity of Earl of Clonmell. Charles Moore, 6th Earl of Drogheda, was created Marquis of Drogheda, and Nicholas Lawless became Baron Cloncurry.

The list of the subscribers in this county to the publication of Taylor & Skinner's *Maps of the Roads of Ireland* in 1777 included the Duke of Leinster, the Earl of Aldborough, the Earl of Drogheda, and Lord Naas, as well as fifteen *gentlemen* of the county including Thomas Burgh, Thomas Conolly, William Eustace, Robert FitzGerald, Thomas FitzGerald, Michael Keating, Richard Neville, William Sherlock, John Wolfe. All of their seats were identified, as were those of non-subscribers such as Joseph Henry of Lodge Park and Rt. Hon. J. Ponsonby of Bishop's Court. Six decades later the enduring dominance of the same families in public affairs was obvious from reports on the County of Kildare Assizes, such as that published in the *Leinster Express & Queen's & King's Counties, Counties Kildare, Carlow, Wicklow, Kilkenny, Tipperary, and Midland General Advertiser* on 12 January 1839. When the County High Sheriff, W. H. Burgh, opened the Court and the Grand Jury was sworn in. It read like a *Who's Who* of the County: Foreman, Hon. Edward Lawless. Members, R. M. O'Ferrall, M.P., R. Archbold, M.P., Sir G. G. Aylmer, Robert La Touche, Robert Borrowes, Hugh Barton, Ponsonby Moore, Thomas Wolfe, Francis Burgh, Charles FitzGerald, Arthur Henry, Baron de Robeck, John Aylmer, George O'Kelly and Alexander Mansfield.

A glance through the loyalist Kildare *Observer* or the nationalist *Leinster Leader*, the two weekly newspapers published in Naas a hundred years ago, reveals the gentry still thriving in what were to be the last decades of their glory. Even if many families lost sons in the Great War, the British military establishments in Newbridge, Naas and the Curragh provided some comfort and constant news. And of course the importance of the military, and of the attendant horse industry, to the economy was obvious. The stratification of society was also very apparent, with the Ascendancy, as the nobility and gentry were called, receiving most attention, the middle class acknowledged, and the lower classes only appearing in the court reports.

That outside these islands ordinary Kildare folk might be propelled to high society was noticed in the New Zealand Herald in 1905. It reported the wedding in London of

Margaret Dowling, the daughter of a man from County Kildare, to the Albanian Prince Albert Ghica, 'a handsome man of about thirty six from a Roman Catholic family, whose members have at various times held the position of Hospodar of Wallachia.'

But even here there was also change, and inevitably the withdrawal of the British army in 1922 altered drastically the social and economic fabric of the county. The contemporary decline of the nobility and gentry was to leave but a few of those once prominent families in their ancestral homes, or with any substantial land holdings. The combination of agrarian agitation and agricultural depression, and the Land Acts of the late nineteenth and early twentieth centuries, ensured the eventual demise of landlordism and the 'big house', while the social and political power of the Ascendancy ended with the Great War and the establishment of the Free State.

The accepted social distinctions of society in times past divided the population into different classes. At the bottom was the landless and impoverished labouring class; next came the different grades of farming folk. On a higher plane were the land owners, stratified by their acreage, and at the top the major landlords, who again were rated by breeding and titles. The latter group generally regarded the city and town folk as trade, and even the professional class were not automatically socially accepted by the aristocracy.

One defining characteristic of a 'gentleman' was his privilege, if offended, of the possibility of initiating a duel. The most celebrated such contest in County Kildare was that at the Hill of Oughterard in 1815, between Daniel O'Connell and John D'Esterre, in which the latter was fatally wounded. However, the earliest account of a duel in this county is from 1744 when, at the County Assizes at Athy, the Earl of Anglesey was prosecuted for assaulting James Annesley from Ballysax and two other men at the Curragh races in the previous September. The men had laid claim to the Anglesey title and estates, and the Earl had described a retainer of Annesley as 'a rogue, a scoundrel and a villain in second-hand finery', but when the man refused to be provoked Anglesey struck him with his whip, which was the traditional invitation to issue a challenge. At the assizes it was said that Anglesey had intended to kill both of the men but they escaped.

A decade later, in 1754, when a dispute arose between the Earl of Kildare and the newspaper publisher, George Faulkner, Kildare forbore to present a challenge as Faulkner was not a social equal, and the Earl should not risk his honour against such a man. By the 1770s a duelling code of honour was firmly established among certain sections of the professions, as already practiced by the gentry and the aristocracy. Gentlemen and soldiers were the main participants in the contests, but artisans, attorneys, merchants, farmers, and even brothel keepers were prepared to risk their lives in defence of their honour.

A politician who questioned the motives of Lord Drogheda, Sir Richard Gore and others in raising regiments to support the Crown's war effort in France in 1759, annoyed Drogheda, and he demanded an explanation in the House of Commons. But that caused furore as it was seen as issuing a challenge in the House, and a duel seemed unavoidable, but there were apologies, and the matter was dropped. The pique and pride of those duelling gentlemen is reflected in the musings of the mid-eighteenth century Abbeyleix born Sir Jonah Barrington: 'In those days the common people ideally separated the gentry of the country into three classes, and treated each class according to the relative degree of respect to which they considered it was entitled. They generally divided them thus: *1. Half-mounted gentlemen: descendants of small grantees of Queen Elizabeth, Cromwell and King William 2. Gentlemen every inch of them: old families whose finances were not in good order. 3. Gentlemen to the backbone: of the oldest families and settlers respected and idolized by the peasantry.'*

While it is not clear which category Barrington saw himself as fitting into, on one occasion his brother William resorted to the gentlemanly privilege of issuing a challenge to a duel. It followed a disagreement at a dinner party at the home of a Captain Gillespie in Athy in 1787. A dispute had arisen between Barrington and a Lt McKenzie, whose regiment was stationed in the town, which escalated into a challenge to a duel being made. It took place in a field beside the river Barrow, where a large crowd gathered. The order to 'Fire' was issued, and both gentlemen fired twice, and missed. Reconciliation was proposed, but Capt. Gillespie intervened and rejected the offer, and harsh words were exchanged between the Captain and Barrington, which ended with the latter being shot dead by Gillespie. Jonah, the victim's brother, took proceedings against Gillespie at Maryborough in 1788, but Gillespie and McKenzie were honourably acquitted.

About the same time as Barrington was musing on his fellow countrymen, the English traveller Arthur Young observed that many of the Irish country gentlemen 'spent all their time in hunting, drinking, fighting, bullying and gambling, surrounded by servants with whom they lived on terms of familiarity, scorning to work, always in debt, roughly dressed in hunting kit, and needless to say, almost illiterate.' He was horrified by the number of brothers, cousins and younger sons that he found 'swarming in gentlemen's houses with nothing better to do than to chase after foxes and hares.' While Barrington's and Young's impressions of the gentry were, no doubt, based on their own observations, they may not have accurately depicted those in this county.

Lord Cloncurry in 1827 also expressed his thoughts on the gentry. He believed that at the great house, 'all disputes amongst tenants were settled, quarrels reconciled, old debts arbitrated; a kind Irish landlord reigned despotic in the ardent affections of the tenantry, their pride and joy.' And interestingly, the patriot John Mitchell writing thirty years later, also had a benign opinion of the class: 'The same powerful assimilating influence which had formerly made the Norman settlers, Geraldines and De Burghs, 'more Irish than the Irish' after two or three generations, had now also acted more or less upon the very Cromwellians and Williamites, and there was recognizable in the whole character and bearing even of the Protestants a certain dash of that generosity, levity, impetuosity and recklessness which have marked the Celtic race.' The Kill-born Fenian John Devoy called for 'the abolition of landlordism. The land of Ireland belongs to the people of Ireland.'

Inevitably, it was Oscar Wilde, whose great-great-uncle in the eighteenth century lived at Elm View, Ladytown, Naas, (and which was later the property of Viscount Allen, whose ancestor had built the enormous brick house at Jigginstown), that expressed the most suc-cinct impression of the gentry. He described them, and their obsession with hunting, as 'the unspeakable in pursuit of the uneatable.'

In more recent times, another acute observer of the class recalled: 'The Anglo-Irish country gentlemen of my day took their colour absolutely from the (British) garrison, not only the patriotic orientation of the latter but their social and mental angle; most younger sons and eldest sons until they inherited their patrimony, joined the fighting services. They vividly remembered the Mecca of the pre-war Curragh, and the smart old days. Unfair and unkind comparisons would have been made (with the Irish army).'

That opinion of the daughter of an Anglo-Irish Royal Artillery officer could almost have been quoted from the society magazine *The Tatler* of 22 January 1936: In a feature describing the annual ball of the Kildare Hunt at Russborough there were photographs of, amongst others, Major J. W. Aylmer, 'former Master of the Kildares, and owns three of their very best coverts. He was in the 4th Dragoon Guards.' Also in the picture are 'Miss Philippa McGillicuddy, Mr Anthony Burke, Mr Pierce Synnott and Mr Roderick

More O'Ferrall.' But the journalist noted, 'Although since the departure of 'The Military' the fields of Kildare are shrunken from their former plethoric state, the Hunt Ball at Russborough House produced no lack of enthusiasts.'

## The Arrival of the Military

A County Kildare gentleman, writing in *The Dublin Evening Post* on 29 May 1821, attributed the tranquility of his area to 'the spirited conduct of the gentry and Catholic clergy who, on the appearance of danger, had all the respectable landholders sworn in as special constables, to the amount of 700 men.' The memories of turmoil in the county, during the 1798 Rebellion and the 1803 Rising of Robert Emmet, were then still fresh, and Catholic Emancipation had not yet been achieved.

Rebel leaders from the county in 1798 had included Lord Edward FitzGerald, and men from lesser gentry families, including Catholic Dr John Esmonde of Osberstown and William Aylmer of Painstown. On the government side were their neighbours, Protestant Sir Fenton Aylmer of Donadea, Michael Aylmer of Courtown, and Richard Griffith of Millicent, who was commander of the yeomanry unit in which Esmonde served. In Sir Bernard Burke's *Dictionary of the Peerage & Baronetage,* published in 1887, John Esmonde was described as having had 'perished a victim of the political disturbance of 1798.'

Both the tranquillity and the economy of the county had been enhanced with a government decision in 1810 to build a barracks for 300 men at Naas. This was followed a few years later with the construction of a barracks for almost one thousand men and 980 horses close to the river Liffey at Newbridge, and the subsequent development of the town across the road from the barracks. Combined with the placing of an extensive encampment on the Curragh during the Crimean War in 1855, the advent of the military was to introduce an additional social hierarchy into the county, as well as a considerable financial input. The gentry welcomed the army officers, many of whom they knew from their own service in the army or militia, or through family connections.

Sociable activities embraced by the gentlemen included membership of societies such as the Masonic Order, of which the 3rd Duke of Leinster was *Grand Master of the Craft, and Sovereign Grand Commander in Ireland.* Or they might join fraternities like the *Kildare Knot of the Friendly Brothers of St Patrick,* an anti-duelling club which met in hostelries, including the King's Arms in Leixlip. Whatever their origin, both the gentry and the military had a common interest in the horse. They were great sportsmen and women, and the horse was an important part of their lives. The meets of the Kildare Hunt Club, and the Punchestown Races from 1850, were major sporting and social occasions, and the men participated in the Turf Club and in the Irish National Hunt Steeplechase Committee.

While the established social status of some families was confirmed by their inclusion in the lists of those who attended the vice-regal court in Dublin, as were members of the Clements, Cane, de Burgh, Crichton and More-O'Ferrall families, the gentlemen might also sometimes socialise with the farmers. The novelist William Makepeace Thackeray attended the agricultural show at Naas in 1842, and afterwards the prize-giving dinner:

'When all the prizes were distributed, a select company sat down to dinner at *Macavoy's Hotel.* At our end of the table we had saddle-of-mutton, and I remarked a boiled leg of the same delicacy, with turnips, at the opposite extremity I observed a large piece of roast-beef, which I could not observe at the end of dinner, because it was all swallowed. After mutton and cheese we were just beginning to think we had dined very sufficiently, when a squadron of apple-pies came smoking in, and convinced us that, in such glorious cause, Britons never fault. We ate up the apple-pies, and then the punch was called for by those who preferred that beverage to wine, and the speeches began. 'The chairman gave 'The Queen,' nine times nine and one cheer more, 'Prince Albert and the rest of the Royal Family,' great cheering; 'The Lord Lieutenant.' His Excellency's health was received rather coolly, I thought. And then began the real business of the night; health of the Naas Society, health of the Agricultural Society, and health all round; not forgetting the Sallymount Beagles and the Kildare Foxhounds, which toasts were received with loud cheers and halloos by most of the gentlemen present, and elicited brief speeches from the masters of the respective hounds, promising good sport next season. After the Kildare Foxhounds, an old farmer in a grey coat got gravely up, and without being requested to do so in the least, sang a song that 'At seven in the morning by most of the clocks, We rode to Kilruddery in search of a fox,' and at the conclusion of his song he challenged a friend to give another song. The jolly frieze-coated songster who celebrated the Kilruddery fox, sang, it must be confessed, most woefully out of tune; but still it was pleasant to hear him, and I think the meeting was the most agreeable one I have seen in Ireland; there was more good humour, more cordial union of classes, more frankness and manliness, than one is accustomed to find in Irish meetings. All the speeches were kind-hearted, straightforward speeches, without a word of politics or an attempt at oratory; it was impossible to say whether the gentlemen present were Protestant or Catholic, each one had a hearty welcome for his neighbour; there were forty stout, well-to-do farmers in the room, renters of fifty, seventy, a hundred acres of land. There were no clergy-men present; though it would have been pleasant to have seen one of each persuasion to say grace for the meeting and meat.'

The observant Thackeray, who stayed with Mr Peter Purcell at Halverstown, near Kilcullen, did not remark on the manners of that gentleman, but he found 'the ladies were as well educated and refined as in England, the meat well cooked, the rooms were clean, and the servants did not talk.'

Of course the life of the gentry was not all hunting, dining or travelling. They could also display their concern for the lower orders, as many of them did during the fam-ine years. Lena Boylan noted in her contribution to Lest We Forget: Kildare and the Great Famine: 'Not to be forgotten or overlooked are the efforts of the local gentry, who aware of their responsibilities, helped in many ways to ease the sufferings of the poor in the town and neighbourhood of Celbridge. In condemning the neglect of the absentee landlords in 1846 Col. Edward Pakenham Conolly of Castletown reminded a Select Committee of the House of Lords that landlords, who have never seen their estates, can hardly have much sympathy for sufferings they have never witnessed.'

In the famine years of 1845-49 the Marquis of Kildare was president of the General Central Relief Committee of all Ireland, which received contributions of almost £84,000 (equal to €8.4m now). Two Church of Ireland relief funds were opened in Celbridge, including the Holy Communion Account, which was funded by offerings collected when the Sacrament was administered in Lord Leitrim's house at Killadoon, Celbridge, and in Mr Arthur Henry's house at Lodge Park, Straffan.

A decade later, when there was a very extreme winter, the Conollys, the Henrys and the Canes of St Wolstan's again led the list of contributors to a relief fund. However, as agrar-ian unrest intensified in the post-famine years, one victim of it was the 3rd Earl of Leitrim who was murdered in county Donegal in 1878. He was head of the Clements family of Killadoon.

Six years earlier another prominent county Kildare grandee, the 6th Earl of Mayo, Viceroy of India, had been assassinated by a lunatic in the Andaman Islands in the Bay of Bengal.

## The Kildare Hunt

For the army officers one of the great attractions of service in County Kildare was the prospect of hunting with the county and neighbouring packs of hounds, and of participating in or attending the race meetings on the Curragh and at Punchestown. The Kildare Hunt Club, which had been established in 1793, was the principal sporting outlet for the officers from the Curragh, Newbridge and Naas barracks. The general officer commanding in Ireland, and the general officers from the Curragh or Newbridge, were usually members. Listed as honorary members, at the end of the nineteenth century, were the Duke of Connaught and Field Marshal Earl Roberts.

Sometimes the officers entertained members of the Kildare Hunt in barracks, as in January 1865 when the 4th Royal Irish Dragoon Guards gave a breakfast to several gentlemen at the Mess in Newbridge barracks. Included amongst the guests were such county notables as the Marquis of Drogheda, the Baron de Robeck, H. G. O'Kelly, and E. A. Mansfield.

The hunting season always closed with the Kildare Hunt Ball, held in the Naas Town Hall from 1860 onwards. In 1867, as reported in the *Kildare Observer,* the rooms there were 'brilliantly lighted with gas and the walls decorated with flowers, evergreens, bannerettes and armorial devices. Caterers from Dublin provided the supper which included every delicacy of the season, including boar's head, Limerick ham, ox tongues, galantines of veal and turkey, perigord of pies, soup, salmon, roast chicken and duckling, lobster, salads, jellies, cream etc. The orchestra was provided by Mr Hanlon's String Band, to which the merry ladies and gentlemen danced waltzes, quadrilles, and the lancers.' The newspaper later carried a full list of those who had attended. While on that occasion the presence of clergy was not mentioned, elsewhere there was a comment that in the diocese of Kildare & Leighlin there were priests 'who ejaculated 'Tally Ho' as often as 'Pax Vobiscum'.'

The April races at Punchestown, always the most important annual event in the racing calendar, were especially important in 1868 as the Prince of Wales made a return visit to the county for the inaugural steeple-chase for the plate in his name (as a twenty-year old captain he had trained on the Curragh in 1861). Three hundred police were drafted in to

*Michael Angelo Hayes's drawing of the Corinthian Cup at Punchestown 1854. The Marquis of Drogheda, mounted, is sixth from left*

Naas to cope with the enormous crowds that came by road and by train to Sallins, where the royal party had also arrived by special train from Kingsbridge. It was a glorious day; the racing was good, and 'the only unpleasant part of the day was the dreadful music of a German band,' according to a report in the *Irish Times* of 17 April. It must have been another great week of parties, not only for the ladies and gentlemen of the county and their visitors, but also for the officers from Naas, Newbridge and the Curragh.

The Prince was in later years to attend two further Meetings of the Hunt races; in 1885, accompanied by his Princess and their eldest son Prince Albert Victor, and in 1904 by King Edward VII with the Queen and Princess Victoria. Both visits were again marvellous social occasions for the nobility and gentry.

A report on the Kildare Hunt Meet at Johnstown Inn on 31 October 1876 revealed that 'The Marchioness of Drogheda never misses an opening meet of these hounds, save for grave reasons....here are the Lady Annette La Touche and party, the Ladies FitzGerald, and the Hon. Mrs Barton on the most charming of grey chargers, Mrs Moore of Killashee, Mrs Kennedy, Miss Kilbee, Miss O'Hanlon, on a beautiful chestnut mare, and hosts more. The Upper House was well represented by Lords Cloncurry, Drogheda etc.' Then the military were listed, by regiments. Inevitably, for most of the ladies and gentlemen of the county, the hunting season was the most anticipated and enjoyable part of the year.

That season was enhanced by the presence of the Duke of Connaught & Strathearn, third son of Queen Victoria and her Prince consort. The Duke participated in stag, fox and hare hunts with all of the major packs of hounds, and he made regular incursions into the county to join the members of the Kildare Hunt. Even if Kildare was described as 'a very artificial country,' it was well supplied with foxes, and on the opening day of the season, at the traditional meeting place of Johnstown 'the carriages of all sorts and shapes were pouring into the village ...amongst the ladies present were the Marchioness of Drogheda who never misses an opening meet of the hounds, and the Ladies FitzGerald and La Touche. The Lords Cloncurry, Drogheda and Clanmorris, and a platoon of military men, led by Gen. Seymour from the Curragh, were there, with Mr Knox and the Horse Artillery from Newbridge. There were parties from the country houses of Killashee, Straffan and the Hon. Charles Bourke's bijou hunting box Roseboro'. Nearly 300 half-crowns were subscribed in cap-money. The Squire of Castletown and Mr Edmund Mansfield represented their dynasties, while Capt. St Leger-Moore was described 'as forsaking his wonted pastimes of tent-pegging, lemons slicing, and all those Indian feats of horsemanship for which his regiment is celebrated, to return for the season.' On another day the Duke of Connaught joined the *Kildares* when they met at Blackchurch to hunt over Johnstown Kennedy, Collierstown Hill, Kilteel, Tinode, Glending, Elverstown, Slieve Rue hill, Arthurstown and Newtown, a long run described as 'desultory.'

For the Meet at Maynooth in March 1877 special hunting trains with horseboxes came from Dublin. It was a very fashionable assembly when the Duke led the field which included numerous lords and ladies, amongst them Lady Maria Fitzclarence, the daughter of the 3rd Earl of Clonmell from Bishopscourt. Her husband Capt. George Fitzclarence RN was an illegitimate descendant of King William IV. Their son, Brig. Gen. Charles Fitzclarence was to merit a VC for service in South Africa in 1899.

As was usual, the hunting season of 1877 closed with a ball in Naas Town Hall, where 'the hunt trophies decorated the walls, there were quality wines, and the music by Liddell's band (worthy of Vienna), and beautiful ladies. The Duke himself was no mere spectator of the gay scene, and he enjoyed the soft glow of wax tapers and the delicious music, as did everyone else. In all, the season was a successful one in a county which was seen as a paradise for hunters, a very Arcady pursuit.'

Two years later when Elizabeth, Empress of Austria, came here for the hunting season, she made an unexpected visit to the Royal College of Maynooth. On the morning when the Ward Union Staghounds met at Batterstown an immense field turned out to welcome the Empress. In what was afterwards described as 'one of the best hunts of the season, the empress stayed with a few other celebrated riders for twelve miles at racing pace until they reached Maynooth, where the stag sailed through a gap in the boundary wall and took refuge in a shrubbery. The President of the College learnt of the unexpected arrival of a distinguished visitor and hastened to offer the empress some refreshments. She spent some time with the college staff, and they invited her to attend Mass there on the following Sunday, which she accepted.'

The Empress also hunted with the Kildares during her visit. When it was known that she was to honour with her presence the Meet at Enfield the town's folk set about decorating their homes with buntings and evergreens, and the fashionable people came in carriages from Westmeath, Meath, Kildare, Dublin and the King's County, to see the Empress. 'William Forbes, Master of the Kildare Hunt, David Mahoney, the hunt secretary, and an imposing assembly of the Kildare gentry waited to join the chase with the empress. They included Lord Cloncurry, Major Lawless, Ambrose More O'Ferrall and the Baron de Robeck, as well as Aylmers, Mansfields, Wolfes, Kennedys, Blackers, and La Touches.' Another indication of the involvement of gentlemen from the county with the military establishment in 1880 was that Capt. Richard St Leger Moore, 5th Lancashire Regiment, from Killashee, was aide-de camp to Major General Seymour, while Capt. the Hon. H. G. F. Crichton 21st Hussars, from Mullaboden, was brigade major.

A few years later both the Kildare Hunt and the Newbridge Harriers had military rank-holding masters when St Leger Moore was the master of the Kildares, and Capt. Gunston of the Harriers. There was also hunting with private packs such as that of Col. Crichton of Mullaboden, near Ballymore Eustace. As well as being secretary of the Kildare Hunt he was a member of the County Kildare Archaeological Society.

Lieutenant Alexander Godley 1st Battalion Royal Dublin Fusiliers, of the Killegar, County Leitrim family, amply displayed the popularity of the Curragh to the officers as a station when he was posted there in 1886. He regarded the Kildare Hunt pack as 'at the zenith of their fame, with Dick Moore (Major R. St Leger Moore) as master.... sport was of the best. It would be hard to find a more delightful field or better sportsmen than hunted in Kildare in that time.'

In his reminiscences Godley recalled some of the Kildare families with whom he socialised and hunted, including the de Robecks at Gowran Grange 'on the edge of Punchestown, a great rendezvous for that historic meeting.' The Baron de Robeck of the day was 'father of the celebrated admiral, and of the late baron, who was a distinguished horse-gunner and subsequently master of fox hounds. His grandson, also a horse-gunner, carries on the sporting tradition of the family.' A daughter of the family had married Captain Bill Tremayne 4th Dragoon Guards, a hunting companion of Godley, and Harry de Robeck, the Baron's eldest son, was 'at Newbridge (barracks) along with other hard-riding gunners.' Godley also recalled an enjoyable afternoon at the Annual Hunt Show on the de Burgh estate at Oldtown, Naas.

Other sportsmen he socialised with included 'Percy La Touche of Harristown, Willie Blacker of Castlemartin, Lord Mayo of Palmerstown, 'Cub' Kennedy of Straffan and Sir Anthony Weldon of Kilmorony, Athy. Lady hunting friends were Eva Beauman from Furness, Naas, who afterwards married Blacker, and Leila Crichton, daughter of Col. Hon. Charles Crichton of Mullaboden,' who married Sir John Milbanke VC 10th Hussars, and who was killed at Gallipoli; she later married General Sir Bryan Mahon.

*General Sir Bryan Mahon, Mullaboden*
*1920. Manager of Punchestown 1925*

Invited to the vice regal balls in St Patrick's Hall in Dublin Castle, young Godley admired the ladies: 'To my mind the Duchess of Leinster stood out among them,' but other ladies connected with county Kildare whom he noticed included Mrs Harry Greer, Catherine Conolly, later Lady Carew of Castletown, and Maud Gonne, who had lived on the Curragh when her father served there with the 17th Lancers.

The officers were regularly invited to the 'big houses' in the county. When the Marquis and Marchioness of Drogheda gave a ball at Moore Abbey, Monasterevan, on 19 January 1876 there was 'a huge attendance.... including Brig. Gen. and Mrs Seymour and aide-de-camp, and officers from the Queen's Bays and Royal Artillery from Newbridge.' After the ball it was arranged that the train from Cork stopped at Monasterevan at 2.45 a.m. to bring guests back to Newbridge.

An indication of the social interaction of the military and the local population can be gleaned from *The Monthly Official Directory of the Curragh Camp & Newbridge*. In that of December 1887, published by Major General the Hon. C. W. Thesiger, Commanding Curragh Brigade, and Inspector-General of Cavalry in Ireland, is included the *Names and Addresses of Gentry, &c., of the Neighbourhood*. The list consisted of some ninety persons, several from the same families, but of which only six came from the list of gentry of 1772, the remainder of the acceptable families having settled in the county subsequent to that date. All of the resident county families, headed by the ducal house of Leinster, and the earls of Mayo, Drogheda and Clonmell, and a sprinkling of lords and ladies, led the field of military and civilian gentlemen who, out of a population of 75,804, were considered to be the social equals of the commissioned officers.

Obviously the hunting field greatly benefited from the military, and the polo ground, cricket pitch, racecourses and shooting parties likewise prospered. The county families attended the seasonal balls and other entertainments in the Curragh Camp, and the reciprocal pleasure of the young ladies and the subalterns added to the excitement. Sometimes weddings ensued, or at least the young bloods enlivened country house entertainments!

The Great War of 1914-1918 caused serious financial problems for the Hunt Club as a large proportion of the costs of the hunt had been met by the military, which was reflected in the club's annual accounts. For the year ending 30 April 1901 military donations had totalled £547. 17.0, while for the war years of 1914-1915 they fell to £50.13.0. Then the club found it necessary to make an appeal for funds, and the Kildare County Council supported the cause. Fortunately, the Kildare Hunt survived the Great War, as it did the disruptions caused by the War of Independence, the eventual withdrawal of the British army from the county in 1922, and the turmoil of the Civil War.

## *The Official List*

Not mentioned in General Thesiger's Military *Directory* of 1887 was the important Conolly family of Castletown, Celbridge, as Thomas Conolly had died a decade before, and his heir was then but seventeen years of age. The latter was killed in South Africa in 1900 when serving as a major in his regiment the *Scot's Greys*. Celbridge also had earlier military associations when Col. George and Lady Sarah Napier came to live at Oakley Park, near the home of Lady Sarah's sister, Lady Louisa Conolly. Col. Napier, who had served in America, and as deputy quartermaster general, fortified Oakley Park during the rebellion of 1798.

Lesser, though long established gentry families such as the Medlicotts of Dunmurry, the Wolfes of Forenaughts, the Kennedys of Johnstown Kennedy and the Sweetmans of Longtown were included in the military directory.

The continuity over the years of the hospitality of the Marquis and Marchioness of Drogheda to the military was again evident in November 1886 when they gave a battue; amongst those who shot over the woodlands at Moore Abbey were HE Prince Edward Saxe-Weimar, Commander of the Forces, with his ADC.

Other county families also entertained the officers. Gentlemen from the 10th and 11th Hussars and 16th Lancers attended a garden party and tournament at Palmerstown, Naas, the home of the Earl of Mayo; and Lieutenant Godley enjoyed the 'great bachelor parties that David Mahony of the Grange (Grange Con), who was secretary of the Kildare Hunt, used to have for the Meets in *Thursday Country*. About twenty of us would sit down in our red evening hunt coats to drink marvellous claret and to listen to Percy La Touche's inimitable stories.'

The officers returned the hospitality of the Kildare families by inviting them to entertainments in the Camp or barracks, and sometimes there was a grand ball, such as that held in the month of August 1887 in the gymnasium at the Curragh Camp. It was made a very grand affair by the attendance of the Prince and Princess Edward of Saxe-Weimar, and numerous high-ranking officers with their ladies.

The local paper reported that the 'neighbouring houses had been filled, (with guests attending the ball) the more the merrier,' and amongst the county families who participated in the evening were the de Robecks, de Burghs, Borrowes, La Touches, Blackers, Moores, Humes and Cosbys. Lt Col. J. A. Connolly VC 49th Regiment, a veteran of the Crimea, was also there. He was resident in the magistrate's house in the Camp (and there he died on 23 December 1888). The gentry mingled with officers from the Grenadier Guards, Royal Artillery, Cameronians, Suffolk and Shropshire Regiments who were then stationed in the camp. The man from the *Kildare Observer* remarked on the brilliance of the gathering: 'the success of the ball was such that the sun had risen before it was over.'

At that time the Kilbees of Canny Court, Gilltown, a minor landed family now gone from the county, were amongst those who enjoyed the hospitality of the military. They are so remembered because of a strange incident, which was said to have occurred as two gentlemen of the family were returning home from a guest-night at the Curragh Camp. The brothers had been introduced to a colonel and his wife, and as they rode back to Canny Court the men set to argue about the charms of the colonel's lady. Dismounting on a diamond of grass at the junction of the Carlow and Halverstown roads, they decided to settle the matter, and drew their pistols. The duel ended with both men dead, and the family at Canny Court was only alerted to the tragedy when the young men's horses arrived home without their riders.

A century after that sad tale a woman of the family, who was back in the area to hunt with the Kildare Hounds, was returning from the Meet when she came to the fatal cross roads. Her horse became agitated, refusing to pass the diamond of grass. A local man managed to calm the horse, and then said to the rider: 'With that blood in you, how could you expect the poor horse to go past that place?', and so she learnt of the family tragedy enacted there long before.

During the drill period of 1891 the presence of royalty at the Curragh again stimulated the social life of the district. HRH the Duke of Clarence and Avondale was there with his Regiment, 10th Royal Hussars. He was the twenty-seven year old bachelor Prince Albert Victor; heir to Edward VII who had himself spent a memorable season in the Curragh Camp thirty years before. The *Leinster Express* of 15 August reported the arrival of the regiment at the Curragh, having come by road from Dublin: 'Captain Wogan-Brown met the prince and his squadron at Moorfield and led them into their camping ground near the Hare Park hospital.'

For Albert's six weeks under canvas on the plain the weather was bad, but he participated in the exercises and sporting fixtures with his fellow soldiers. Games of polo were played at some of the country houses, and at the coming of age of Thomas Conolly of Castletown in September the prince joined the nobility and gentry of the County at the celebrations.

Albert succumbed to complications following influenza in January 1892, and the *Leinster Express* noted, 'In Kildare and Dublin the Duke of Clarence was well known, having many friends. He had visited Punchestown about six years ago with his father, and recently was stationed at the Curragh with his regiment where he won the respect and esteem of everyone with whom he came in contact.' The military and the gentry were, of course, greatly involved in the visit of Queen Victoria in 1898. She stayed at Carton, and visited St Patrick's College, Maynooth.

The enlargement of the social scene in County Kildare due to the presence of the army was undoubted. If the officers and their families reaped most benefit from the hospitality of the many big houses, they reciprocated by providing eligible young men, lavish barrack entertainments and frequent professional displays on the training grounds. Almost all sections of the population were at some time or another entertained by the military, even if it was only by the playing of a military band.

Undoubtedly, equine sports were the main recreational pursuit of the officers, one that they shared with the gentry. Early in 1899 the Hussars held their Point-to-Point at Barretstown Castle, the home of the Borrowes family near Ballymore Eustace, with the Earl of Mayo, Lt. Col. de Robeck, Col. Crichton, Sir Kildare Borrowes and Mr T. J. de Burgh as stewards. When the Army point-to-point had been held a short time before it was at Cockeranstown, on the land of three other County Kildare gentlemen, Lord Cloncurry, Sir Algernon Aylmer and Sir Fenton Hort of Hortland. At the opening of the hunting season in November 1899 it was accepted that the hunt, like many others, would suffer as so many of the gentlemen had gone to fight the Boers in South Africa.

Another common ground for the gentry and the military was the cricket field. At Naas the Shamrock Cricket Club was established in 1860, and over the following decades the game flourished with clubs at Athy, Monasterevan, Moone, Narraghmore, Newbridge, Celbridge, Halverstown and Kildare. There were also 'big house' teams at Straffan, Kildangan, Eyrefield, Harristown and Bishopscourt, but the main centre was at Oldtown, Naas, where the County Kildare Cricket Club had absorbed the old club in 1871. The Moore, de Robeck, Borrowes, Blacker and Aylmer families were active members. Inevitably, the cricket field suffered from the withdrawal of the British army in 1922; it was to have a devastating impact on the sport in Kildare, from which it never recovered.

What might be termed another 'county club', the County Kildare Archaeological Society, did survive the traumatic year of '22. Lord Walter FitzGerald had established the Society in 1891, with his father the Duke of Leinster as president. The membership included virtually every County family, and the Society's journal was to become a highly regarded publication. The excursions of the Society were reported in detail in the local newspapers.

In 1907 Lord Walter's co-secretary of the Society, Sir Arthur Vicars, K.C.V.O., F.S.A., *Ulster*, Office of Arms, Dublin Castle, was embarrassed when on 6 July the Irish crown jewels were found to be missing from the castle. Believed to have been stolen by a group of socially prominent dissolutes, the jewels were never recovered, and Vicars lost his appointment. His nephew Pierce Gun O'Mahony, who was *Cork Herald of Arms*, was found drowned in the lake at Grange Con, County Wicklow, in 1914. Vicars were living at Grange Con, the home of his elder half-brother Pierce O'Mahony, when it was burned by the IRA, and from there he moved to Kilmorna, the old Mahony house in County Kerry. Misfortune followed him to Kilmorna, where, on the suspicion of being a spy, he was shot dead by Republicans in April 1921, and the house was also torched.

The conjunction of Lord Walter FitzGerald's sudden death in 1923 and the changed political situation might have caused the demise of what could be seen as an ascendancy Society, but fortunately that did not happen. The *Archaeological Society* is still thriving, and members from the remaining gentry families have continued as office holders. In recent times Gen. Sir Eric de Burgh and Lt Col. Charles Clements were Presidents, and the Canadian born Dr Richard Aylmer 16th Baronet of Donadea was a council member.

## The Families

Leading the aristocracy of County Kildare was the Duke of Leinster, the premier nobleman in Ireland, whose family, the FitzGeralds, had been in the county for almost eight hundred years. He was the largest landowner in Kildare, and his seat at Carton, Maynooth, within its magnificent parkland, was one of the finest in the country.

Lord Edward FitzGerald, the hero of the 1798 rebellion, is now the best-remembered member of that Anglo-Norman family, which since 1316 had carried the title Earl of Kildare. The prominence of the FitzGeralds had reached its peak in 1766 with the elevation of Edward's father to the rank and title of Duke of Leinster.

Landed families settled in Kildare since the seventeenth century included the MacWilliam Bourkes, who had the title of Earls of Mayo from 1785; their mansion at Palmerstown, Naas, stood on almost 5,000 acres. Another family from the same root was the de Burghs of Oldtown, Naas, whose ancestor Thomas Burgh, engineer and surveyor-general for Ireland, had settled there late in the seventeenth century. His brother William, of Bert, Athy, was the great-grandfather of General Sir Ulysses de Burgh, 2nd Baron Downes, who had been aide-de-camp to Wellington in the Peninsula, and later surveyor-general of the ordnance.

The Weldons of Kilmorony, Athy, the Lattins of Morristown Lattin, Newbridge, and the Borrowes of Gilltown and Barretstown, Ballymore Eustace, were respected landed and military families, also tracing their origins in Kildare to the unsettled times of the seventeenth century.

Thomas Conolly of Castletown, Celbridge, has been described as 'the greatest figure in the history of the eighteenth century horse racing and breeding in Ireland,' and as 'Father of the Turf Club.' In 1761 he purchased a house in Kildare town, to be adjacent to the Curragh. Another celebrated supporter of the sport was the Marquis of Drogheda, Monasterevan, who served as Steward of the Turf Club from 1866 to 1892.

But when the bi-centenary of the club was celebrated in 1991, and *Horses, Lords & Racing Men,* the history of the Club by Fergus D'Arcy was published, it reflected changed times. It noted that Major John de Burgh of Oldtown, Naas, a member of the Turf Club (and one of the few remaining gentry), had a decade before accepted that without increased commercial sponsorship for the sport, it would not have prospered.

Though only established in the county since the eighteenth century the Clements of Killadoon, Celbridge, the Mansfields of Morristown Lattin, Newbridge (who had married into the Lattin family), and the de Robecks of Gowran Grange, Naas, held extensive estates as well as lands elsewhere in the country. The founder of the latter family was a Swedish nobleman who had served with the French army in America in 1781; after marrying an Irish heiress he settled here, and his descendants included many distinguished soldiers and sailors who intermarried with other county families.

If not great military families, the La Touches of Harristown and the Lords Cloncurry of Lyons also provided brides for army officers. In 1865 Emily Maria La Touche married Lt. Gen. Hon. Bernard Matthew Ward; and the wife of Valentine Browne, the 2nd Baron Cloncurry, was a daughter of Major General George Morgan.

At Moore Abbey, Monasterevan, which they inherited through marriage at the end of the seventeenth century, the Earls of Drogheda had 16,609 acres. They lived in great style, and were enthusiastic supporters of the turf. The third Marquis of Drogheda was lieutenant colonel commandant Kildare Rifles, and Ranger of the Curragh from 1868 to 1892. Ponsonby Moore of Moorfield, Newbridge, who owned much of the land developed there by the military in the nineteenth century, was a son of the 5th Earl of Drogheda.

A comparative newcomer to the county was John Henry Scott, the 3rd Earl of Clonmell, who in 1838 married Anne, the daughter of General Sir Ulysses de Burgh, 2nd Lord Downes, of Bert, Athy. Clonmell purchased Bishopscourt, Straffan, and added the 1,958 acres there to his 25,688 acres in six other counties. Bishopscourt had been built in the last decades of the eighteenth century for the Kilkenny born Rt. Hon. John Ponsonby, Speaker of the Irish House of Commons.

The Cloncurry family of Lyons, originally the wealthy Roman Catholic, and later Protestant, Lawless business family from Dublin, had one remarkable daughter. Emily, a poetess who died in 1913, wrote a volume of poetry *With the Wild Geese,* and several novels. Years before that Charlotte Burgh of Bert, Athy, had satirised the Lawless family in verse. She was inspired at the theatre when she saw Sancho Panza being tossed in a blanket. Observing that Lord Cloncurry (whose title was then new, and the memory of his ancestor's woollen trade still fresh) had not yet arrived at the theatre, she wrote:

'Cloncurry, Cloncurry, come here in a hurry,
To look at this comical squire,
They toss him quite high, but between you and I,
Good blankets have tossed you much higher.'

The only Roman Catholic families in the county gentry were those of Mansfield, More O'Farrell, Sweetman, O'Kelly, and Wogan-Browne. The de Burgh family, which included several Protestant clergymen, did have one Roman Catholic member, Hubert, a priest (1830-1901).

## As it was in 1900

The pages of the *Kildare Observer* for the year 1900 illustrate the importance of the aristocratic and gentry families in the administration, military, sporting, cultural and social life of the county. Of course the fact that the *Observer* was an establishment and loyalist newspaper ensured that the landed families, the garrison and the Church of Ireland were given generous coverage.

Despite the Land Acts of 1870, and later the agricultural depression and agrarian disturbances of the 1880s, the landed families remained the dominant social class. The departure to or return from the Boer War of the men of the FitzGerald, Conolly, Moore, de Burgh, de Robeck, and other landed families was given special notice, as was the support for the men at the Front by their ladies. Led by Lady Mayo, an unending series of bazaars, fetes, raffles, concerts and other social activities were organised to raise funds for 'comforts' for the troops. Mrs St Leger Moore and Mrs More O'Ferrall issued appeals for the Royal Dublin Fusiliers, while Mrs Claude Cane of Donacomper supported a concert at Naas for the Soldiers' Widows & Orphans Fund. She recited Kipling's The *Absent Minded Beggar*, and Lady Albreda Bourke from Palmerstown provided flowers for the decoration of the hall. Society weddings were described in detail in the *Observer*, such as that of a member of the Weldon family in London, when two paragraphs were devoted to listing the wedding presents. Similarly, the funerals of notables were given detailed coverage, with full lists of the mourners.

Some of the gentry were prominent in county administration, such as George Wolfe of Forenaughts. He was a magistrate and a member of the committees of Kildare Infirmary and of Naas Union, as well as being a member of Kildare County Council. Other councillors were Ambrose More O'Ferrall of Kildangan, and Lord Frederick FitzGerald from Carton. Lord Mayo and John de Burgh of Oldtown were magistrates.

*Col. St Leger Moore of Killashee*

The Meetings of the Kildare Hunt, the Hunt Show, and its annual steeplechase at Punchestown, were the major sporting events of the year, and the Master of the Hunt was generally from a county family. The Punchestown committee embraced gentlemen of the Mayo, Moore, La Touche, De Robeck, Mansfield, Blacker, Kennedy and Tynte families, while their house-guests for the race meetings merited listings in the newspaper.

There was a Grand Concert at the Curragh Camp in March 1900 in aid of Lady Robert's War Fund. Lt. Col. Richard St Leger Moore, Commanding the 17th Battalion Imperial Yeomanry, was the patron of the evening. Of course the ladies contributed, with Mrs Claude Cane, from St Wolstan's, taking the place for two items on the programme of Mrs de Burgh from Naas, who was ill. Col. St Leger Moore, from nearby at Killashee, was, to quote journalist Hector Legge, 'well known for the big dinner parties he gave, opportunities, no doubt, for fair young ladies to meet exciting young military men.' That the gentry might also be mentioned in the press for less commendable reasons was evident when the Canes of St Wolstan's featured in a *Kildare Observer* report of a court case which they took against Miss Norma Borthwick, who was accused of having uttered a £1 forged cheque with intent to defraud. The accused, addressing the court, said that she had been engaged by Major and Mrs Cane to give Irish lessons to Major Cane and his daughter, and that the disputed cheque had been signed by the Major. She was found not guilty.

The ladies of the county actively participated in local organisations and charities: the Secretary of the Kildare Society for the Prevention of Cruelty to Animals was Mrs St Leger Moore, while the committee consisted of ladies of the FitzGerald, Mayo, Cloncurry, Borrowes, Clements, Lattin, and Wolfe families, many of whom were also involved in the Horticultural Society.

In the doldrums month of August 1900 it was reported, 'Mr Eugene Kelly had become tenant of Castletown, and it was by no means unlikely that the pet poodle of his wife, which has created by the treasures of its wardrobe such a sensation in Paris, will also visit Ireland.' A couple of months later it was noted, 'The Countess of Mayo had quite recovered from her recent accident, and has again resumed hunting. The Earl of Mayo has arrived at Stratford Place, and Lady Mayo will shortly go to London.'

The newspaper *Gossip Column* noted the departure of individuals or couples to London or elsewhere abroad, and if they were wintering abroad that was also revealed. Social visits were noted, such as that 'the Sweetmans of Clane were expected to entertain Sir William and Lady Butler, as he was a brother of Mrs Edmund Sweetman. Lady Butler had painted *The Roll Call* and other military subjects, and he was author of *The Great Lone Land,* and *The Wild North Land*. A former Commander in Chief in South Africa, he had been educated at Clongowes Wood.'

An important adjunct to the 'big house' was the indoor and outdoor staff. In a survey of six of the houses in this county it was found that all of the people employed in both 1901 and 1911 were literate, and as the Census Returns for those years show, upper staff tended to be Protestant and British, while many of the lower staff were Irish Roman Catholics. Personal servants were 93% Protestant and only 7% Catholic.

At the Earl of Drogheda's Moore Abbey, Monasterevan, in 1901 fifty-five persons worked on the estate, of whom eighteen were Catholics, as were three of the eleven house staff. John La Touche at Harristown, who was a Baptist, employed six indoor ecumenical staff: two Church of England, and one each from the Church of Ireland, Church of Scotland, Presbyterian Church, and Catholic Church; a decade later there was no Catholic there. Lady Mayo at Palmerstown had thirteen servants, including a cook, scullery maid, kitchen maid, three housemaids, two ladies' maids (one Swedish and the other English), an

English butler and housekeeper, two footmen and a hall boy, of whom two were Catholic. At Oldtown in 1911 the de Burghs had a staff of five, three of whom were Catholic, and at Aylmers of Donadea Castle three of the indoor staff of seven were Catholic. The Mansfields at Morristown employed eleven staff, all of whom, like the family, were Catholics.

## Traumatic Times

When the newly crowned King George V and Queen Mary visited Maynooth College in July 1911 there was a great assembly of the aristocracy, led by the Lord Lieutenant and the Countess of Aberdeen; the ducal house of Leinster was represented by Lord Frederick FitzGerald (his nephew Maurice, the 6th duke, was unwell and rarely seen in public). Other 'county' present were George & Mrs Mansfield of Morristown Lattin, Newbridge, Nicholas Synnott of Furness, Naas, and Mr & the Misses Mooney of Leixlip Castle.

Derick Barton of Straffan, in his autobiography published in 1989, looked back over ninety years, and reminisced on those halcyon days. 'Before the Great War,' he recalled, 'with the army still in occupation on the Curragh, in Kildare and in Newbridge, there was an enormous following (of the Kildare hunt) and it has always remained a vivid picture in my mind, these seventy years later, there was generally a guest or two from the garrisons at the Curragh or Newbridge (staying at Straffan). I am not sure if their horses came with them, there was ample room in the stables and for the soldier grooms in the rooms overhead or they may have come by the train to Straffan Station.'

Hector Legge, a former editor of the *Sunday Independent*, reminiscing on his boyhood in Naas, recalled happy days on the courts of the County Kildare Cricket & Tennis Club before the bleak years of the Great War, when no annual general meeting of the club was held from May 1914 until June 1919. However, 'in the years before the war the County Kildare Club was one of the outstanding sports centres in Ireland. In cricket, lawn tennis and hockey, its members were to the fore. At that time the British Army was strong in Ireland. There were barracks in Naas itself: *Royal Dublin Fusiliers*; in Newbridge: *Royal Field Artillery*, and the many cavalry and infantry regiments on the Curragh. For the officers the County Kildare Club offered golden opportunities for them to play cricket and

*Lt Col. Charles Clements, Queen's Hussars*

tennis. Young ladies of those families made many a marriage with army officers through the tennis court. It was the age of what was referred to as *the gentry*.'

Another traumatic time for the gentry was the Rising of 1916. Two members of the Kildare Hunt, who, in later years, recalled their memories of the outbreak of the rebellion, were Lt Col. Charles Marcus Lefevre Clements M.C. and Percy La Touche. Clements remembered that on Easter Monday he had accompanied his mother to visit the wife of Brigadier Portal who lived in a rented house near Newbridge. They were to attend the military sports after lunch, but the lunch was cancelled, as the brigade was very busy. By teatime they knew that there was trouble, and the trains were no longer on schedule. Brigadier Portal hired a car to take his visitors to Naas, as it couldn't go any further, and a telegraph was sent to the coachman at Killadoon to have the side-car sent to the hotel at Naas to collect them. On the way home the young Clements saw troops, with their equipment and guns, lined up along the wall of Oldtown on the Sallins road.

Another gentleman from Kildare, and a Member of the *County Kildare Archaeological Society*, who had first hand experience of the rebellion was Capt. Henry Eliardo de Courcy-Wheeler A.S.C., of a family settled at Robertstown since early in the nineteenth century. On 29 April 1916 when Patrick Pearse surrendered in Moore Street, Dublin, de Courcy-Wheeler was accompanying General Lowe. He had earlier taken the surrender of the Royal College of Surgeons, and he also had the task of accompanying the Countess Markievicz, who was a distant cousin through marriage, as a prisoner to Dublin Castle. Percy La Touche and a neighbour drove up to Dublin on Tuesday 2 May 1916 'taking revolvers with them just in case.' They found the streets full of troops, armoured motor cars, ambulances and machine guns, causing La Touche to speculate, 'When racing might be able to start up again!'

A contemporary, and no doubt an acquaintance of the gentlemen just quoted, who was serving in the British Army was to die tragically at home soon after Dáil Éireann had approved the Anglo-Irish treaty. Twenty-three year old Lt John Wogan-Browne, of Keredern, Naas, an only son, was shot by a group of men who robbed him of the regimental pay as he returned from the bank to the barracks in Kildare in February 1922. His ancestors were the old Roman Catholic families of Wogan and Browne of Clongowes and Rathcoffey.

Those troubled years also affected the *County Kildare Archaeological Society*, many of whose officers and members were from the landed class. The Council noted in the annual report for 1922: 'we regret to report that last year was one of great trial to the Society.' They were not referring directly to the political situation, but to the fact that over the previous decade there had been a decline in membership. In common with other Antiquarian Societies, their finances had been much reduced, and the cost of publishing the *Journal* was becoming difficult.

If the withdrawal of the military was to have disastrous effects on the local economy, the demise of the gentry was also to have repercussions. Gradually the hunting field and the cricket and hockey clubs, and more seriously, the congregations of the Protestant churches, were being adversely affected. Soon the 'big houses' and walled estates began to come on to the market, and a rise in unemployment was inevitable. In time some of the 'big houses' became religious institutions or colleges, then hotels and golf courses, while others were demolished. It is fortunate, for historical and architectural reasons, that in recent years wealthy Irish families have purchased and restored some of the houses, and repaired the crumbling boundary walls. More importantly, several of the estates remained with the original families, and these, as well as those of the departed gentry will now be considered.

# 2

# The FitzGeralds

In ancient times the area that is now County Kildare was the territory of the Gaelic tribes, the Uí Faelain, the Uí Failge and the Ui Muiredaig. With the coming of the Anglo-Normans in the late twelfth century new territorial divisions were made, and in the thirteenth century County Kildare was one of the shires created. Much of it was to become the demesnes of newly arrived adventurers, some of whose descendants were to occupy dominant roles in the county for hundreds of years.

For over seven and a half centuries the Anglo-Norman family of FitzGerald was the most aristocratic and important in the county. They claimed descent from the Gherardini of Florence through one Lord Otho, who had first settled in Normandy, and went from there to England in 1057. His great-grandson Maurice FitzGerald came from Wales to Ireland in 1169, at the instigation of Dermot Mac Murrough, king of Leinster, and he was to be the progenitor of the Kildare family.

A century later the continuity of the family was almost terminated when a fire in Woodstock Castle threatened to engulf the cradle of the infant heir. Fortunately one of the family's tame apes came to the rescue, snatching up the boy and taking him to safety. Subsequently the FitzGerald crest was to depict two such mammals, and a nineteenth century poet wrote:

*The Arms of the Duke of Leinster*

For centuries now hath the monkey been
In his dark unconscious rest;
But emblazoned still is his image seen
In the proud FitzGerald's crest.

The family produced many notable men, such as the 1798 patriot Lord Edward, and in earlier times, Gerald the 'Great' (8th) Earl of Kildare, 'Silken' Thomas, the 10th Earl, and Gerald, the 'Wizard' Earl: *Geroit Mac Geroit Mhic Geroit Iarla Cille Dara,* as identified by the scribe compiling the *Annals of the Four Masters* in the seventeenth century.

His father, Gearóid Óg, the 9th Earl, died in the Tower of London in 1534, and his half-brother, 'Silken' Thomas, was executed with his five uncles at Tyburn three years later for involvement in what was to be known as the Kildare Rebellion. The 9th Earl had spent his teens in Rome, and in later years he accompanied the Knights of Rhodes to battle against the Moors. On the accession of Queen Mary he was restored to his earldom and he returned home. Elizabeth FitzGerald, his youngest daughter, was taken to England by her mother following the execution of 'Silken' Thomas, where she remained permanently. Absorbed into the household of her distant relation Princess Mary, she was later a maid of honour to Queen Catherine Howard. A celebrated beauty, Elizabeth was immortalised in poems written by the Earl of Surrey, and in her portrait, painted about 1560, which is now in the National Gallery in Dublin.

Eleanor, the daughter of the 8th Earl of Kildare and his wife Alison Eustace, had an eventful life. She was twice married, for dynastic reasons: firstly to Dónall McCarthy, Lord of Carbery, County Cork, and following the rebellion of the 9th Earl in 1534, she married Manus O'Donnell to strengthen the Geraldine alliance with the northern chiefs. Eleanor was involved in the smuggling of the Geraldine heir to safety in France, and later described as 'being but a woman' she was pardoned by the Crown. In County Kildare Gerald, 11th Earl, is remembered in folklore as the 'Wizard' Earl. Local tradition related how the Earl and his retinue lay in an enchanted sleep beneath the Rath of Mullaghmast, and that he emerged every seven years to magically gallop his ghostly white horse around the Curragh! He had articulated his Irish identity in 1580 when he asserted 'All you Englishmen are joined in one and an Irishman can have no right or justice at your hands.'

Over the following centuries the FitzGerald family had the normal bouts of good and bad fortune. Henry, the 12th Earl, whose wife was a daughter of the Earl of Nottingham, had no male issue, so the title went to his brother, William the 13th Earl. He was unmarried, and was lost at sea in 1599; then the title went to his cousin Gerald, the 14th Earl. He was married to a Nugent cousin, and they were unfortunate when their son, the 15th Earl, died at the age of nine. The title then went to their cousin George the 16th Earl, who married a daughter of the Earl of Cork, and their son was Wentworth, who in time was the 17th Earl. His heir in due course was John, the 18th Earl. Unfortunately, again he had no heir and consequently the title went to a cousin, Robert, who as the 19th Earl was an eminent statesman. His wife was a daughter of the Earl of Inchiquin, and James, the only surviving one of their four sons, was the 20th Earl. He married a daughter of the Duke of Richmond, and was in time advanced to the rank of Marquis, and then to that of Duke of Leinster.

## Florentine Origins

The coincidence of the Reformation with the demise of the lordly FitzGerald family, following the revolt of 'Silken Thomas' in 1534, had enabled the emergence of a new dominant order. The new arrivals included the families of Eustace, Sutton, Aylmer, Bermingham, Wellesley and Colley, as well as English officials such as the Alens, who were the recipients of confiscated monastic lands and houses; some of them also benefited from the redistribution of confiscated land belonging to the Earl of Kildare and his supporters.

'In the aftermath of the Geraldine rebellion,' wrote Mary Ann Lyons in the *Journal of the County Kildare Archaeological Society,* 'almost at once County Kildare underwent cataclysmic changes. It lost its principal dynasty. It was stripped of its liberty status, its monastic houses were suppressed, and it was left in a partially wasted state as a result of the Geraldine rebellion and subsequent raids mounted by neighbouring Gaelic elements. And, as a result of the removal of the Earls of Kildare and the closure of the monasteries, it witnessed the emergence of strong, independent-minded County gentry, some of whom were to fiercely oppose the restoration of the 11th Earl of Kildare in the early 1550s'.

To-day it is sobering to know that none of the families which assumed prominence in those turbulent times are now resident in the county, or of the lesser families of Kerdiff, Sherlock or Flatisbury, all of whom had also then prospered. While the ducal house of Leinster was again dominant from the eighteenth century onwards, it finally collapsed in the mid twentieth century. Members of the Aylmer, Eustace, Sherlock and Wogan families were also still in the county in the early twentieth century.

A visible expression of the opulent lifestyle of the FitzGeralds in the early eighteenth century may be seen in the Ulster Museum, Belfast. It is the twenty-eight piece silver-gilt toilet service commissioned in 1722 by the 19th Earl of Kildare for his wife, Mary O'Brien, daughter of the 3rd Earl of Inchiquin, on the birth of their third and surviving son, the future Duke of Leinster. Engraved with the arms of the FitzGeralds, 'it was used at the levée, an eighteenth century fashion which involved the entertainment of guests during the process of dressing the lady of the house. The porringers contained liquid foods such as possets (a hot drink of milk with wine and spice) presented on the salvers,

*Emily, Duchess of Leinster*

while the boxes and pincushion stored pins and accessories for the costume. Perfumes and lotions were kept in the flasks, and whisks and brushes then removed the powder and cosmetics from the completed ensemble.'

The 19th Earl, who held the office of Lord Justice in 1714, undertook the building of a mansion at Carton to replace the old family castle at Maynooth. Thirty years later when the proposed Demesne was mapped, including a Deer-park, it contained 861 acres.

James FitzGerald, the 20th Earl, commenced in 1745 the building of Leinster House in Dublin. Soon after its completion in 1754 James was given the freedom of the city and presented with a circular gold freedom box. The Leinster arms were engraved on the lid, and on the base the Arms of the City of Dublin. That same year the Earl was involved in a dispute with the newspaper publisher George Faulkner, and though a duel was considered, the Earl forbore to present a challenge as he considered Faulkner was not his social equal, and he should not risk his honour against such a man. The freedom box remained in the Kildare collection until 1984, when it was sold.

James was created Marquis of Kildare in 1761 and Duke of Leinster five years later. He also commissioned a silver gilt service, which surpassed that of his father. It was a dinner service consisting of 240 pieces. His Duchess was Emily, a daughter of the Duke of Richmond, whom he married when she was fifteen years of age. She was one of three sisters who, in the late eighteenth century, were the chatelaines of the neighbouring great houses of Carton, Castletown and Oakley Park, Celbridge.

## Kildare's Travels

In 1766, at the age of seventeen, William Robert FitzGerald, Lord Kildare, the second son of Emily and the Duke of Leinster, set out on his Grand Tour of Europe, which was to last three years. His tutor, Mr Bolle, accompanied him, and at various places on his travels his cousin Charles Fox, or other relations and friends, joined him. During his travels William wrote to his mother very frequently, and in his first letter, from Lyons, he described a visit to a Carthusian monastery: 'They are a set of very religious monks that never speak to one another but Monday and Thursday. They have each of them a cell, which contains two rooms and a little garden for them to work in. They all dine together of a Sunday and must not speak. They never eat meat or broth made of meat; they eat nothing but fish and eggs, and that is given them through a little door made in the wall.'

Then he travelled on to Marseilles from where he intended going by sea to Naples: 'I believe we sail tomorrow. I dread the sea very much, for I went out a little way to see our ship and was very sick. But I hope after the first day it'll go off.' Luckily, he had a pleasant voyage of eleven days and was soon installed in Naples where he was to spend the winter. He became immersed in the social life of the city, attending balls and concerts, including a supper at the palace of the Princess Francavilla:

'Everything was very magnificent. But one course, and dessert, served very well and clean; silver plates, dishes, all very clean, which I never saw in France, and change knives and forks... I can't say much for the beauties of this town, as I think except for five or six that are tolerably pretty the rest are hideous.' The opera he found was 'as magnificent beyond anything I ever saw. People take their boxes by the year, and you go and make your visits to them there. Nobody ever thinks of listening except when there comes a favourite tune; then they are so attentive that you might hear a pin drop...'

From his lodgings the traveller could see Vesuvius, 'smoke in the day time, at night a redness in the sky.' A few weeks later 'things started to liven up; Mount Vesuvius makes a great noise and flings up a great deal of matter; I am still in hopes of having an eruption.'

William was still in Naples at Christmas. On the eve of the feast he visited several of the churches in the city: 'I was much disappointed, as I expected to have seen a much finer procession and better music, all the churches better lighted. I was at one of the best, where they performed High Mass. After they had done, they carried our Saviour in procession round the church, and then put him in a manger that was built up on purpose for that occasion, where there was a number of puppets dressed like shepherds, and the Virgin Mary and Joseph. After our Saviour was laid in the manger, it really was quite a puppet show as that common music stood playing there, drunk.'

By April 1767 FitzGerald was in Rome where he visited the churches and palaces, and 'had the honour of kissing the pope's toe (N.B. it was very sweet). He is a very agreeable old man and is very fond of having strangers presented to him.' Later he again saw the Pope: 'in his robes in the church he is very like an old woman; he looked like a very cross one to-day, for he had just received an account of the King of Spain's banishing the Jesuits out of his dominions.'

The city of Florence, which Kildare found 'to be an agreeable place enough,' was to him of special interest as it was believed that it was there that the FitzGerald ancestors, the Gherardini had originated. But during the high summer William was in Turin 'in a suffocating heat... and fleas by the dozen, and killed about a third part, so you may imagine there is left sufficient number to eat me up.' He had also 'got to be as lousy as a person can well be; but I am now in hopes that I have got quite rid of them, as I have had fifty killed, and have filled my head with Spanish snuff, which is a sure cure.'

William was in Venice in October 1768: 'the most disagreeable place I ever was in, especially as I am quite alone and have not a house to go to.' But he was soon fortunate to meet 'two fellow Irish, Mr and Mrs King, who made those few days agreeable, she being a very agreeable woman'.

When he reached Vienna in January he was happy to find that 'at present a number of Irish officers are in town; so you may be sure I am not much alone. We have here a Count Mahony, a brother-in-law of the Countess that is at Naples, who is ambassador from Spain, who is one of the most agreeable, civil, obliging men I ever met.' In March he was in Prague from where 'he would be willingly off on the 16th, as the 17th is St Patrick's Day, and this town swarms with Irish, and there is an Irish convent of Franciscan friars who have a feast that day.'

While he was abroad William had been elected a Member of Parliament for Dublin, and by the age of twenty-four he was married. He inherited the title of 2nd Duke of Leinster when his father died in 1773. But that did not prevent his association with Margaret Leeson, the celebrated Dublin Madame of the eighteenth century, whose business prospered for thirty years. She could boast that she entertained such clients as a Governor of the Bank of Ireland and a Lord Lieutenant, as well as several gentlemen from this county. Born Margaret Plunket, she adopted the name Leeson from an English merchant who had for a time supported her, and who had lands in County Kildare, 'with an excellent house, and beautiful demesne, where we lived in perfect tranquillity and content...' Mrs Leeson wrote in her *Memoirs* of a bed for which 'I had put myself to great expense, the furniture being of new muslin, richly spangled. It was kept locked up, being designed for the Duke of Leinster, who, after all the preparation, never came.'

Eventually she fell on hard times, and to raise some funds she wrote her story, but not to embarrass her former patrons she referred to them by their initials only. The memoirs,

*William FitzGerald, 2nd Duke of Leinster*

published a decade ago, were edited by Mary Lyons, a bibliographer in the British Library. Her diligent research enabled many of Leeson's clients to be identified, such as David La Touche, Governor of the Bank of Ireland, whose family was for a considerable period owners of Harristown House, near Naas. Another eminent client from this area was Joseph Leeson, first Earl of Milltown, who built Russborough House.

In contrast, in 1795 when it was being proposed that a seminary for the education of priests should be established near Dublin, the Duke welcomed the suggestion that it should be at Maynooth. Lady Louisa Conolly of Castletown also interested herself in the matter. On the 20 April of the following year the foundation stone of the Royal College of St Patrick was laid by the Lord Lieutenant, and *The Hibernian Journal* reported 'His Excellency was accompanied by His Grace the Duke of Leinster, the Earl of Clonmell, the Rt. Hon. Thomas Conolly, several other dignified characters and gentlemen, whose countenances bespoke the most pleasing sensations of the mind, at seeing this testimonial of liberality in the legislature and government of Ireland demonstrated to their Roman Catholic brethren.'

Afterwards the dignitaries were invited to dine at Dublin Castle, and later Clonmell came to note the fact in his diary: 'Lord Camden laid the foundation stone of the popish seminary at Maynooth. I attended him with the Chancellor and the other two chief judges, and we dined at the castle with several popish bishops, and other Trustees. (N.B.) A very new scene in this kingdom, and important in its consequence.'

A high opinion of the Duke was expressed by Thomas Rawson, the agriculturalist from Athy, who thought poorly of some land owners. In his *Statistical Survey of the County Kildare*, published in 1807, he wrote: 'All Ireland, and the county of Kildare in particular, has much of its vital strength drawn away by absentees. The late, much to be regretted, 2nd Duke of Leinster was a lover of his country; he almost constantly resided at his magnificent seat of Carton, where he set an example of hospitality and benevolence, and by every humane attention to the wants of the industrious people, to whom he gave constant employment, and charitable assistance, he called aloud on the nobility and gentry of Ireland to imitate so great and good example.'

## The Fecundity of the Duchess

Emily, the mother of William Robert, the 2nd Duke, had given birth to seventeen children, of whom the fifth boy, Lord Edward, affectionately called Eddie, was her favourite. When she was widowed in 1773 Emily married the children's tutor, William Ogilvie, and they had two children. A not very flattering opinion of Ogilvie was that 'he was originally a drummer in a Scotch regiment. From the drum he preferred to a writing-school in a village in the county Kerry, from whence he was translated to a writing-school in Dublin, from whence he was preferred to the Duke of Leinster's nursery in the capacity of private tutor to his children. Whilst in this station, he did His Grace the honour to get three or four bastards on the person of his duchess, to which said bastards the present Duke has the honour to pay £10,000 each, and now Mr Ogilvie having made an honest woman of his mother, that worthy and sagacious nobleman, his stepson, repays the many obligations which he had conferred upon him, by submitting himself wholly to Mr Ogilvie's management and direction.'

The second Duke, Lord Edward's brother William Robert, had inherited great debts from his father. He also had to provide portions of £10,000 each for his three sisters who married, as well as making financial arrangements for another who did not wed, and there were further substantial obligations towards his brothers. Nevertheless he managed to be able to afford the comfort of some expensive courtesans, such as Mrs Leeson and her contemporary Mrs Porter, 'who now figures away in a neat furnished house in Mark Street, where she has a resort of the best company; particularly a noble duke who is passionately fond of her; her chief delight, is boasting to her votaries of the presents she receives from her 'noble slave', as she terms him, particularly a diamond ring, a late offering of his, to this frail beauty.'

Fortunately, when William Robert married Emilia-Olivia, the only child of Lord St George of Headford Castle in county Galway, she brought him considerable property, the sale of which assisted in improving their financial situation. As that marriage was blessed with two sons and six daughters there was again a keen necessity to provide for them. One of the girls married a neighbour, John Joseph Henry of Straffan, a member of a Dublin banking family.

William Robert died at Carton in 1804 and he was buried at St Brigid's Cathedral, Kildare. Historian Elizabeth FitzGerald later wrote, 'So well loved was he by all classes and all parties in Ireland that it was said the funeral procession stretched the whole length of the Curragh'.

Isabella, his fourth daughter, a couple of years before she married a French nobleman in 1809, had commenced writing *Some accounts of the first twenty years of my pilgrimage on earth*. She remembered her uncle Lord Edward as being:

'particularly manly and distinguished. His features were regular and his fine blue eyes beamed with spirit and enthusiasm from under his long eyelashes. The beauty of his teeth and the sweetness of his smile were heightened by the bright healthy glow of his manly complexion which almost concealed his being slightly marked with the small-pox. He was one of the first to cut his hair short and leave off powder, which was very becoming to him; and as he was fond of swimming in the river, it proved very convenient; his hair was of a dark brown colour and had sufficient wave in it to make it sit prettily with little care besides constant washing which Lord Edward was almost the first to introduce. So that Cropped head as it is called became a party distinction.'

Lord Edward served with the 19th Regiment in America, and when he returned home in 1783 he brought with him his Negro man-servant Tony Small, who had been responsible for saving his life in the battle of Eutaw Creek two years before.

FitzGerald had been influenced by the philosophy which had led to the French Revolution when he visited Paris in 1792, and he hoped that with the aid of the French a similar revolution could be successful in Ireland. May Day 1798 was to be the day of Rising, but the authorities had infiltrated the movement and a reward of £1,000 was offered for information on Lord Edward. His refuge in Bridge Street, Dublin, was raided, and he was wounded, but not before he had killed one of his attackers. Lodged in Newgate prison, he died there from wounds on 4 June. The burial of Lord Edward in the vaults of St Werburgh's church in Dublin was, Stella Tillyard writes, 'arranged by his aunt Louisa Conolly. It was a botched affair that took place at midnight; she had collected what relics she could of Edward, including a locket of his hair'. The late burial hour was to prevent any exhibition of popular feeling, which it was feared would certainly have occurred.

After Lord Edward's death Tony Small accompanied the widow Pamela to Hamburg. Pamela was the illegitimate daughter of the Duc d'Órléans. Tony had established a relationship with Julie, the nursemaid to the FitzGerald children, and they soon settled in London where he died within a few years, it was said of a broken heart.

Lord Edward is the only member of the family to be officially remembered today. He had spent his early-married years in Kildare town, and in the bi-centenary year of the 1798 rebellion a monument to commemorate his residence there was erected in the town square.

*Lord Edward FitzGerald by Hugh D Hamilton*

## The 3rd Duke of Leinster

When Augustus Frederick, at the age of thirteen, had succeeded to the title of 3rd Duke of Leinster in 1804, he was then the only Irish duke, and both premier marquis and Earl of Ireland. Years later he was described by the indefatigable Elizabeth Smith of Baltyboys as 'good natured, but his duchess (a daughter of the Earl of Harrington) noisy, his son rather nice, his daughter ugly.'

However, decades later, *The Leinster Express* in February 1839 published a critical article on the Duke:

'The first step was one which gave signal offence to his countrymen, who are ever of Sheridan's opinion, that Justice is a lame, hobbling beldame, who can never keep pace with generosity. He at once sold Merrion House, a magnificent mansion occupying an entire side of the nobler square of the same name, and took decided steps to enable him to liquidate the large debts with which the extravagant habits of his father had left his patrimony encumbered. For honourable purpose he diminished his state to the narrowest bounds which his high rank would allow; and bore firmly and proudly the imputation of meanness, rather than sully his conscience by suffering the lowliest creditor of his family to be wronged of one farthing. When his brother, Lord William Charles O'Brien FitzGerald (1793-1864) had to pay heavy damages in a case of crim. con. (adultery), Augustus Frederick paid the sum of twenty thousand pounds.'

The *Leinster Express* also noted that 'On a recent occasion when the duchess's jewels went missing, drawings of them were sent to all the ports here and on the continent; a fortnight after they were restored as mysteriously as they had gone. Circumstances, however, had transpired in the interim, which fixed their abstraction with painful certainty, on a near relative of his Grace's. The presumed guilty person, who had for years been dependant on the bounty of the Duke, was obliged to withdraw to France. The Duke further demonstrated his magnanimity when he undertook responsibility for the daughter of the culprit.'

Leinster was described as 'leading a quiet life in the bosom of his family. He plays the violoncello, two or three soirees a week, with leading musicians of the metropolis as guests.' And he did not neglect Carton, where 'every clock in his princely seat is regulated by a time piece in the hall, and if he observed two minute variation between any of them, an express is sent to Dublin for the watchmaker to come. Agriculture is his great passion and excellent farm houses have been built for the tenants.' Carton house had then been remodelled, and alterations were underway at Kilkea Castle, where 'the wretched cabins of forbidding appearance on the estate were demolished and new substantial dwellings built, laid out in streets, and with yards and gardens.'

# 3

# A Black Sheep

*Lord William's Story*

Unfortunately, the Duke of Leinster's younger brother Lord William Charles-O'Brien FitzGerald did not merit much acclaim. The year 1815 was to prove a traumatic one for the FitzGerald family: Leinster House, their classical mansion in the Dublin, was sold to the Royal Dublin Society, and an embarrassing court case was in the offing. It came before the Hon. Judge Mayne and a special jury in the Dublin Court of Common Pleas on the 27 February 1816 and damages of £20,000 were claimed against the twenty-three year old Lord William.

*The Times* reported on the 2 March:

'CHRISTOPHER TAAFFE ESQ. V. LORD WILLIAM FITZGERALD: Mr Whitestone, stating the case for the plaintiff, observed that his client, Christopher Taaffe, was a man of most respectable rank and connexions. In 1800 he was married to a lady of birth and fortune, by whom he got a dower of £5000. He was then in affluent circumstances, having a clear income of £4000 a year, beside considerable property in stock, in the counties of Mayo and Sligo. This most amiable woman survived her marriage not much longer than a twelvemonth. Knowing her value, duly estimating the comforts which are alone to be enjoyed in virtuous matrimony, it was not unnatural that he should in three or four years after her decease, feel anxious to supply her place by a partner of equal claims to his affection and confidence. He found, in 1806, in the person of Miss Honora Burke, of Glinsk, sister to the baronet of that name, as he imagined, a most suitable successor of the former Mrs Taaffe. His circumstances were then improved. His stock had increased and his income amounted to the full sum of £5000 a year. He was not parsimonious in securing the independence of Miss Burke against all casualties; his settlement was most ample, though she brought him a fortune of no more than £2000. From that period to 1813 the parties lived in a state of the most enviable felicity. In the beginning of that year, their enjoyments were, for the first time, interrupted by some pecuniary difficulties, which became at length so embarrassing as to give birth to an alteration in their domestic arrangements. In short, it had been deemed expedient to lop off some expensive appendages to the country establishment, and change their residence for a short period to Dublin, where they were contented with a few apartments, and a contracted retinue.

In the early part of the spring of 1813 they had taken lodgings in Kildare-street. Shortly after the intimacy with Lord William FitzGerald, the defendant, who was, as the jury were appraised, a member of the house of Leinster, and brother to the present duke, commenced. Between the plaintiff and this young nobleman a friendship appeared to be soon cemented, than which nothing could be more ardent on one side, or sincere and confident on the other.

Indeed, so close and familiar had this unlucky acquaintance become, that it gave rise to an interchange of kind offices, such as is not often witnessed among the nearest relatives, and many of the periodical difficulties of the plaintiff were promptly and cordially removed by the advances of the defendant. That no suspicion on the part of the injured husband could grow out of this intercourse, was a conviction enforced by two circumstances, supposing human nature to be as frail as corruption itself, and taking it for granted that a man should have no confidence in a wife who had given him, during a connection of seven years, the most incessant and unequivocal proofs of her fidelity and affection. He alluded to the wretched state of the defendant's constitution at the period alluded to, and the almost hopeless infirmity of Mrs Taaffe's health. From a disease in the knee, the latter had become an object capable of exciting more of loathsomeness than amorous appetite, and a general debility of constitution had rendered the latter a subject better calculated to move the pity than alarm the jealousy.

There was another circumstance which tended powerfully to restrain the suspicion of the unfortunate husband, if indeed it could ever be awakened under the existing circumstances. There was at this time living with Mrs Taaffe, a lady whose name he was compelled to mention, but could not mention without presenting to the imagination of every individual who knew her, every quality and attraction of mind and person which adorns and illustrates the female character. He alluded to Miss Blake of Ardfry, the aunt of Mrs Taaffe. For this lady the defendant appeared to have contracted a strong attachment; so strong, indeed, that it led to some remonstrance's on the part of the plaintiff, who thought, and candidly, and like a warm and honest friend, represented to Lord William, that a union between him and the object of his supposed affection, however it may be encouraged by the beauty and accomplishments of the lady, was peculiarly imprudent for both parties. To the remonstrance's of Mr Taaffe, the defendant was, or affected to be deaf, and he insisted on a prosecution of his suit. Was not this another powerful allayer of any suspicion that a man, not afflicted by the inquisitorial jealousy of a Spaniard, could possibly have felt? Did it not give Lord William FitzGerald an irresistible claim to the confidence of the plaintiff and to the most familiar intercourse with his family? The infirmities of Mrs Taaffe gave her an imposing excuse for urging the expediency of a journey to London, to seek fresh and more salutary advice than she had received among the faculty of Dublin. When she spoke of a journey of health, she set aside all arguments her husband could use. Precarious as were his circumstances, he never thought of expense or inconvenience where there was a prospect of administering to her real or imaginary comforts.

Towards the close of 1813, an expedition to London was planned by her. Lord William FitzGerald could not have remained unacquainted with the design. He was soon in possession of the intentions of the unhappy woman (or was more probably the person who originally suggested the scheme) and he proposed, as his health was also in need of some adventures in the way of locomotion or advice, to be of the travelling party. There could be no objection to his proposition, and after some arrangements, Mr & Mrs Taaffe, Miss Blake (Mrs Taaffe's aunt), Lord W. F. and a young child embarked for Holyhead. In some time they arrived in London, and after the plaintiff had put his wife under the protection of her brother, Sir John Burke, he returned to Ireland to adjust his distracted and embarrassed affairs. From Mrs Taaffe after his return he had almost daily communications. Nay, on some occasions, he received two letters on the same day, fraught with every sentiment expressive of love for him, concern at their separation, affliction for his difficulties, and solicitude for her children. With such address indeed did she carry on the delusion which it was her whim or her conceived interest to practice, that long after her guilt, he supposed he had in her the most faithful, the most considerate, and fondest of wives; some months rolled on, and at length some friend suggested to him that her delicacy of health did not require a continued residence in London. He imparted to her the suggestion, and she in her answer attributed it to the malevolence of some hidden enemy. He endeavored to remove her impressions, and her reply was, that she conceived her life would be the forfeit of an effort to remove, but at the same time she protested her determination to obey if he demanded her return. He of course was rendered mute by such an appeal. Thus matters remained until August 1814. At that period Lord William FitzGerald was understood to be at his brother's at Carton, having returned from England for a few days, and Mr Taaffe, on his coming up to town from his country residence, called to see him, and enquire for the friends he had left after him in London. Mr Taaffe had not been timely in his visit, for Lord William had departed two days previous to the call, and departed for London. The next account that the unfortunate plaintiff had either of Lord William or the ill-fated partner of his guilt was, that their criminality was no longer equivocal, and that they had fled to the continent, taking with them not merely the child (a female) who had gone from Ireland, as already stated, but a girl six years old, who was placed by her father at a public school in England. On hearing these sad tidings what were his feelings?

The sun went forth, but Conrad's day was in,
And the night cometh, ne'er to part from him.

In short, said the learned counsel, since the receipt of the fatal intelligence, the plaintiff is an exile from the comforts and consolations of society. For a whole year had the adulterous pair revelled in the enjoyments of travel, change of scenery, and uninterrupted passion, passing throughout as man and wife. About August 1815, they returned to England, and took up their residence at Hastings. The unhappy plaintiff soon discovered their retreat, and he then sent after them – not to recover his wife, for he no longer claimed any such being, but to recover his children. Those he did not obtain. A special messenger, whom he had sent over, had received her answer that they would not be surrendered. 'You see us here,' said Lord William FitzGerald, 'the children are safe, and will not be delivered up; we live as man and wife; and all we ask of you is not to expose us.' The anguish of the unfortunate Mrs Taaffe, at the interview with this messenger, appears to have been exquisite.'

*View of the Law Courts looking up the Liffey, by James Malton, 1799*

*The Times* report continued:

'The Revd Thomas Costello proved the marriage. He further deposed that the parties lived in the most perfect agreement and harmony. Henry Corr, Esq., was next called. He stated that he never knew any people more reconciled or happy. The plaintiff's wife was a woman of rare fascinations of person and manners. She had three children previous to 1810, and since witness understood that a fourth was born.

John Nolan, Esq., the third witness, was the brother-in-law of the plaintiff, whom he knew since he was boy. He had opportunities of observing his conduct towards his wife and hers towards him, and nothing could be more affectionate or endearing. He was asked whether he conceived Mrs Taaffe to have been a fond mother, and he answered the in the affirmative. He was the first witness to whom a question was put in the shape of cross examination. The solicitor General, on the part of the defendant, seemed anxious to learn from him, whether he had known Lord William FitzGerald and Mrs Taaffe to have been together at different parties, and in various vehicles, previous to their departure from Dublin, and without the presence of her husband; and whether he heard any report connected with Lord William's intimacy with Mrs Taaffe, which was injurious to her reputation? The witness said he certainly heard some reports which he discredited, but that he himself observed no familiarity or intercourse in the way the Solicitor-General alluded to which would awaken his suspicion.

George Aikins, the messenger above alluded to, was produced to prove that he had been dispatched in quest of the children by Mr Taaffe; that he met Lord William and his old mistress at Hastings; that on seeing him she evinced extreme anguish; that she and Lord William refused to deliver up the children; and that the latter mentioned that himself and Mrs Taaffe lived as man and wife, requesting of witness at the same time not to disclose the secret to any person whom he may meet at Hastings. Mark Byrne, Esq. (one of the jurors) deposed that he had met Mrs Taaffe and Lord William FitzGerald, in the South of France, living as man and wife.

The Solicitor General, for the defence, called several witnesses: Michael Doyle knew, and was in the service of Lord William FitzGerald, in the summer of 1813. He knew at the same time Mrs Taaffe, when he drove her to and from Kildare Street; saw and knows her often to have been in the carriage with Lord William. He, Lord William, always ordered the carriage to call at her lodgings when they were going out together, when Lord William walked up from Leinster House to take his seat in it. Once Lord Sydney Osborne got in at the same time, and he drove them all to the gardens in Rutland Square; it was then the dusk of the evening. Lord William was very young at the time, and Lord Sydney Osborne, he believed, was still younger. Mr Taaffe saw him one evening in waiting, spoke to him, and gave him some money to drink. He drove them (Lord William and Mrs Taaffe) one evening to Mr Verschoyle's at four or five miles from Dublin. He believes Mr Taaffe was in Dublin at the time; afterwards he brought Mrs Taaffe and Lord William from Mrs Verschoyle's. When they drove off from Mrs V's, it could not be less that 10 o'clock; the second time he drove them to Mrs Verschoyle's was about the latter end of September, or beginning of October. He saw Mr Taaffe at the coach door; first time he excused himself from going; he went neither of the times he drove Lord William and Mrs Taaffe.

Richard Verschoyle, Esq. recollects inviting Mr & Mrs Taaffe, and Lord William FitzGerald, in the summer of 1814. Mr & Mrs Taaffe, and Lord William had left their tickets at his house; this induced him to give the invitation. Lord William and Mrs Taaffe came, but Mr Taaffe did not. He does not recollect inviting them at any other time; they left his house together about 10 o'clock. He believes Mr Taaffe was in Dublin at the time; he sent an apology for not being able to come himself. He could not say that he heard rumours at the time about Lord William and Mrs Taaffe. He had met them in Dublin at different times, and after saw them in England.

Thomas Scott, a servant to the Duke of Leinster, was servant to His Grace in 1813. He said that Lord William resided at Leinster House that Spring, and that he knew Mrs Taaffe and her husband, he saw her and Lord William frequently together, he saw them walking in the streets together with her arm under his, and he saw them more than once. He remembers going to Carton to a breakfast given by Lord William. Lord William was particularly attentive to Mrs Taaffe at breakfast, he saw them a second time at breakfast at Carton. They walked together on the grounds after breakfast.'

On his cross examination by Mr North, Scott deposed, 'that on the journey from Holyhead to London, Mrs and Miss Taaffe, Miss Blake, and his Lordship rode inside; Mr Taaffe condescended to ride outside with the driver. They put up at a hotel, the first three days, when Mr Taaffe took a private lodging for his wife, and immediately left London for Ireland. This lodging the lady changed twice or three times after. He, the witness, saw them together in Lord William's carriage until about 4 January 1814'.

The Jury withdrew for about half an hour and returned with a verdict. 'Their Lordships were of the opinion that adultery was fully proved, and Damages £5,000 were awarded.' So ended the report of the proceedings in *The Times*. The money was paid by Lord William's agent to Mr Taaffe's agent, who handed it over to Taaffe's brother-in-law Mr Nolan, who in turn paid it to the petitioner, and he swore that no part of the money went back to Lord William. Thus concluded the official report on a most expensive and embarrassing episode in the annals of the ducal house.

Lord William was again mentioned in the newspapers in 1830 when a general election was being held. It was usual that the county of Kildare was represented by a member of the FitzGerald family, but as the election date approached *The Times* commented that: 'It is remarkable enough, however, that Lord William FitzGerald has not yet addressed his constituents, and if persevered in, I should not be surprised if the ties which so long connected the Leinster family with the county of Kildare should receive a shock, which even His Grace's property and the name of FitzGerald, a popular name in Ireland, would find difficult to remedy.' Other candidates for the county included Sir William Hort, and Mr Moore O'Ferrall. A month later the paper noted that 'Lord William FitzGerald has neither come nor written to the county, although the election is at hand.'

Lord William retired from the representation, and the next mention of that gentleman in the newspaper was in February 1832. He was then wintering in Rome with 'about 800 English, a number much less than in preceding years. With the exceptions of the Earl of Pembroke, Lady Clare, the Countess of Coventry, and Lord William FitzGerald, there are few of any notoriety among them. The society, however, although limited, has been extremely agreeable and pleasant this winter. The House of Torlonia, to which all the English who transact business in the bank of that firm are invited, has given repeated splendid soirees. Their entertainments, however, are not over select, and on the last *recevimento* evening a great sensation prevailed on the entrance of the fair companion of an Irish nobleman into the rooms. She was unaccompanied by her lord. Many respectable English ladies instantly retired.'

Lord William died in 1864 at the age of seventy-one. He was not brought back to Maynooth for burial.

## A Royal Occasion

Lord William's older bother, Augustus Frederick, 3rd Duke of Leinster, Grand Master of the Freemasons, Ireland, had with the Lord Lieutenant and other dignitaries, the honour to receive King George IV, his god-father, when he came to the special Royal Meeting at the Curragh Racecourse in 1821.

Lady Glengall later recalled the occasion: 'The Duke of Leinster arrived at the Curragh with this dreadful intelligence; the king had been smitten with an internal affliction! A hurried conference was called and one of the stewards admitted that 'one thing has been omitted....I mean a water closet; I humbly propose that 'Artists' may be forthwith summoned from Dublin to erect one before his arrival.' The Duke arranged to go to Dublin to procure the 'artist', and soon this man arrived, but wanted to know 'the dimensions of the seat and other appearances.' 'The usual dimensions would suffice', said the Earl of Mayo, 'as his majesty, though corpulent, was finely turned'.

His Majesty was pleased with the 'shrill and howling' reception he was given by the Irish peasantry, but just as the racing got under way 'His Majesty was obliged to bolt. His Grace the Duke of Leinster was called for, as he had undertaken to do the honours of the new erection. Exeunt the duke, walking first with a white wand, then the king, and immediately behind, the doctor.' Before leaving the Curragh the king presented the Duke of Leinster with a gold whip to be awarded to the owner of the best horse in Ireland, weight for age, and he requested that the race should be run for the whip annually.'

Over a decade later, in August 1839, when the foundation stone was laid for the Celbridge Union Workhouse by the Duke of Leinster, the *Leinster Express* reported 'the ceremony over, His Grace on leaving the ground was loudly cheered. In the evening Mr Regan entertained a few friends at the Hibernian, in Mr Bean's (the proprietor) usual good style, on the cloth being removed, the health of Her Majesty Queen Victoria was proposed and drunk, and also that of His Grace the Duke of Leinster, Col. Conolly, the Lord of the Soil, etc.'

Augustus-Frederick had inherited a gross rental of £36,320, but the estate was so heavily encumbered that he was under severe strain to support his dukedom. His status, and expenses, were further raised in 1849 when Queen Victoria paid the family the honour of staying, with her entourage, at Carton during the royal visit to Ireland. Ireland's Premier Duke, who was Lord-Lieutenant of the County, and Grandmaster of the Freemasons of Ireland, had made elaborate preparations for the visit of the queen and her consort. To ensure an enthusiastic reception for the royal couple, Carton estate was thrown open to the public. Special trains brought crowds of people from Dublin to Maynooth, and the newspapers later reported that 'all morning the roads leading to the town were crowded with carriages and cars of all types, and pedestrians. Every vantage point was occupied. The royal party came by the Liffey valley, preceded by an advance guard and two mounted servants in royal livery; files of the 8th Hussars were immediately before and after the two royal carriages, which were accompanied by postillions and outriders. All along the road cheering people greeted the queen, while the students of Maynooth College came to Leixlip to raise their voices.'

It was a gloriously fine day, and Carton was said to look marvellous with its marquees on the lawn behind the house, and two military bands to entertain the guests. Exactly at nine o'clock the royal standard was raised as Queen Victoria and her consort alighted from their carriage to be greeted by the Duke and Duchess at the main door of the house. Dressed in pink and blue silk, patriotically covered with Limerick lace, and carrying a parasol, her majesty took the Duke's arm to be led about the garden, and afterwards to lunch in a marquee; then the tenants danced jigs, to the music of the pipes, which the queen found most amusing. She was particularly impressed by the thick blue coats, short breeches and blue stockings of the men, and the manner in which one dancer had his hat tilted over his ear! Later the Duke's long Bianconi car was brought round, drawn by two horses, and the Duke and Duchess led the royal couple around their demesne; the general

*Carton House, Maynooth from* The Graphic *Oct 24, 1874*

view from the ancient tower was enjoyed, and then the shell cottage by the lake was visited. Crowds of people followed the party, riding, running and driving, which the queen enjoyed: 'Their yells,' she later noted, 'sounded so different to the English cheers.'

It was intended to bring the visitors back to the house by the water, and a boat with the royal standard was moored by the cottage. But the Queen saw that her time was limited so she accepted the Duke's invitation to travel back by an outside car; this was her first experience of such a vehicle, and she was very taken with it. The Duke was so happy with the success of the visit, and the Queen's regard for the Irish car, he had one built in Dublin and sent to her at Windsor.

A ballad commemorated the event:

> Sure when the queen was over here she said she'd like her health to thrive,
> So the darlin' duke of Leinster thought he'd thrate her to a dhrive.
> She got on his outsidher, and before she had gone far,
> 'Be me sowl', says she, 'I like the joultin' of yer Irish jauntin' car.'
> So she had one made in Dublin and she wrote to Mister Maher
> To send out Larry Doolan for to dhrive the jauntin' car.

In 1870, when there was a threat of evictions on part of the lands of the Duke of Leinster in the town of Kildare, a journalist from *The Illustrated London News* visited there. He found that the agent for the ducal estates instigated the trouble, and that the town's folk did not at all associate the Duke with the threatened evictions (which did not take place), 'for he was universally spoken of as one of the best landlords in the sister kingdom.' Nevertheless, the journalist saw that the condition of some Leinster tenants 'was most pitiable.... a more starving, ragged, ill-housed community than the occupants of the wretched mud-cabins that lined one side of one of the principal streets in Kildare, it was hardly possible to conceive.'

A decade later Dr Samuel Chaplin, who tended to the people of the town, wrote 'Kildare is differently circumstanced from any of the other towns in the county, with very few resident gentry. Thanks to the kindness of His Grace the 4th Duke of Leinster a large portion of the labourers found employment during the past winter, and even now are employed at Rathangan, Athy and Maddenstown.'

According to Hall's *Ireland: The Scenery & Character* (1841), to honour the occasion in Kildare of the coming of age of Charles William FitzGerald, who was destined to become the 4th Duke of Leinster, 'the inhabitants made a huge bonfire on the top of the Round Tower, when some daring fellows contrived to climb to the summit.'

As Marquis of Kildare in the famine year of 1846 he had been President of the General Central Relief Committee, but he did not succeed to his titles until 1874, and two years later he was listed as the proprietor of 70,462 acres, with an annual valuation of £47,710.

And there were good times, as Daisy Fingall later recalled: 'They had big parties at Carton during those years. King Edward and Queen Alexandra, then Prince and Princess of Wales, had been there during their Irish visit of 1885, although not to stay. And the Visitor's Book is full of important and interesting names. But I often stayed there when they were alone or when there were only two or three of her particular friends: Emily Lawless and her brother Freddie, who used to play the organ, Arthur Paget, Lord Elcho, whom we called Count Hugo, Dunraven, Bully Oliphant, Bee Cloncurry, Lady Eva Bourke, now Lady Dunraven, are some of those I remember.'

His successor, Gerald, the 5th Duke, was listed in the *Curragh Camp & Newbridge Directory*, in 1887, the year he succeeded to the title. That his marriage to Lady Hermione Duncombe, who was regarded as the most beautiful woman of her day, was not a happy one, she revealed in a letter; 'What I resent is that though K. had no more wish than I have that we should live *martialement*, he still insists in sleeping in my room for fear that the servants may think!' Nevertheless they had four children, two who were destined to be dukes of Leinster.

## A Rival for the Dukedom

The ancient house of FitzGerald has been the subject of many strange stories of both fact and fiction, but few of them have been as extraordinary as that of the man from the

*Gerald, 5th Duke of Leinster and first president of the County Kildare Archaeological Society, 1891*

United States who claimed that he was the rightful heir to the Dukedom of Leinster, and who died at the age of eighty in 1979. Michael Estorick has written a splendid account, *Heirs & Graces: The Claim to the Dukedom of Leinster*, (Weidenfeld & Nicolson. 1981).

Maurice FitzGerald, who said he was born in 1887 and had been educated at Eton, emigrated to the United States in the early years of the twentieth century. There he joined Buffalo Bill's Circus, and afterwards continued to find employment with horses. By the time he married a rich wife he had changed his name to Charles Tyler, and later he was again to change his name, and also to marry twice more. But he sometimes claimed that he was really Maurice FitzGerald and Duke of Leinster, as he had relinquished his title in favour of a more suitable younger brother. Some substance to this claim appeared to be his regular supply of money from an unknown source in Ireland. He spoke of his early life at Carton and Kilkea Castle and of his school days at Eton. He recalled his attendance as a page at the coronation of Edward VII in 1902. Eventually some newspapers took up his story, and after his death a book was published on the subject. His eldest son, Leonard, put forward a claim in the form of an application to the Lord Chancellor in London for a *Writ of Summons* to the House of Lords; the claim was rejected and in 1976 it was withdrawn.

But who was this Maurice FitzGerald, alias Charles Tyler? It would seem that he was the son of the wife of the bandmaster of the 1st Battalion, King's Royal Rifle Corps, Frederick John Tyler, but not a son of the bandmaster. Fellow officers in that regiment were three of the FitzGerald brothers, sons of the 4th Duke of Leinster.

Bandmaster Tyler was a fine musician, and a popular fellow with his colleagues, including the FitzGeralds. In their period of service together in India the friendship between the Kildare gentlemen and the musician and his wife prospered, and during the voyage home it was rumoured that relations between Mrs Tyler and Lord Charles FitzGerald exceeded friendship. Early in 1887 she gave birth to a son, and his lordship was believed to be the father. The infant was named Charles Tyler. Lord Charles emigrated to America.

The real Maurice FitzGerald, son of the 5th Duke of Leinster, was mentioned in the *Kildare Observer* in August 1901. In a report that the King and Queen were planning a visit to Ireland, it was said that 'Kildare's young Duke of Leinster, who is in his 15th year, occupied a seat under the gallery of the House of Commons on Tuesday night, where he was brought by his uncle, Sir Howard Vincent. Mr Swift Mac Neill, it is said, told him thrilling incidents in the career of his great-grand-uncle Lord Edward FitzGerald.

Maurice, a nephew of the three officer brothers, was a tall, fine looking man, and as a boy had been a page at the Coronation in 1902. However, due to illness he had been withdrawn from Eton, and at the age of twenty-one, when he attempted to murder his valet, he was found to be seriously mentally disturbed. Lodged in a private hospital in Scotland, he remained there until his death in 1922. Brought home for burial, and being then 6th Duke of Leinster, his funeral was private, and no mention of his death was made in the newspapers. The second son, Lord Desmond, had been killed in 1916 in the Great War, and so the youngest brother, Edward, inherited the title of 7th Duke of Leinster.

The question remains, how did Maurice FitzGerald/Charles Tyler succeed in convincing people that he was the real heir to the Leinster titles, who had abandoned his birthright in favour of a brother? Possibly it was from his mother that Tyler had heard stories of the Kildare family, which she herself would have gathered from the three FitzGerald officers. It was also thought that he could have visited Carton and Kilkea. Initially he may have seen himself as a genuine member of the family, except for the unfortunate fact that he was illegitimate. In time, it would appear, he believed himself to be a real FitzGerald, and he assumed the mantle of a lord.

It was Lord Edward, the 7th Duke, a younger brother to the ill-fated Maurice, who was to cause the disintegration of the family estate of Carton. A high-living gentleman, he made a deal with Sir Harry Mallaby-Deeley MP, who owned the *Fifty Shillings Tailor* chain of stores: Sir Harry would pay off Edward's debts of £67,500 and make him a tax-free allowance of £1,000 a year for life, and in return he would receive all the income from the estates after Edward inherited the title. As the 6th Duke was then only in his thirties it seemed a good deal, but fate intervened, and the Duke died within a few years, and Edward inherited. The income from Carton then passed to Sir Harry, and for the next fifty-four years the 7th Duke, was to live in much straightened circumstances, being declared bankrupt no less than three times. When the property came into the possession of Mallaby-Deeley there was immediate concern at Carton, where an unmarried aunt and uncle of the Duke lived. Sir Harry made a statement:

'Some four or five years ago I was asked to purchase these reversionary rights and I refused. About twelve months later the offer was repeated. I said I was still not very keen on purchasing, but that I was prepared at a price to buy. I was told by expert advisers that the price I proposed to pay was perfectly ridiculous, meaning that my offer was, in their opinion, far too high. As far as I know the estate is being run as usual. I am bearing the whole expenses of the estate, and my agreement with the duke is that everything should be carried on exactly as it has been in the past. It is still open for the repurchase by the duke's family.'

The Duke, through his secretary, gave his views:

'I can say that the Duke is in no way parting with his birth-right, as he has an option to re-purchase within a certain number of years. The sum for repurchase is £350,000 and not £400,000 as has been stated. The estate of the Duke of Leinster is worth more than £2,500,000, and, in addition, the heirlooms are valued by him at the best part of £2,000,000. Carton costs £8,000 a year to maintain, and the annual income from the estate is more than £45,000. The employees on the estate are still in the Duke's service and there is no need to worry about the place changing hands. Sir H. Mallaby-Deeley is in daily touch with the Duke, and it is only a question of the solicitors making the necessary arrangements for the completion of a deal which will be satisfactory to both parties.'

However the Duke himself was worrying about the situation in Ireland where the Civil War was being fought; he announced that he would do his bit for his country by joining the Free State Army. He believed that it was his duty to render whatever assistance he could when he found his country was in need of his service. But his intentions did not come to fruition. At Carton things were not so promising, and Lord Frederick, who had been elected to Kildare County Council on its formation in 1899, was in charge in the absence of his nephew the Duke. He admitted to the press that, as an economy, he had received instructions to reduce the staff. Nor did the FitzGeralds ever reclaim Carton.

The sad last days of Carton were described by Terence Dooley in the journal of the *County Kildare Archaeological Society* in 1995: 'When Edward married Rafaella (Davidson-Kennedy) in the early 1930s, Lady Nesta FitzGerald was living alone at Carton, courtesy of Mallaby-Deeley. Her only company was a handful of servants. Her surroundings were sparsely furnished and callers few and far between. The glory days of the ascendancy and their big house had truly gone forever. By 1949, the upkeep of the house was too great a burden on what was left of the Leinster income. It was, thus, sold in that year to an English brewer, Lord Brockett, for £80,000, ending a long and distinguished connection between the FitzGeralds and the area of Maynooth. As for Lord Edward FitzGerald, he was to spend much of his life living in a succession of council flats and bed-sitting rooms, acquiring for himself the title Bed-Sit-Duke.'

Married four times, one of his wives was Joan McMorrough Kavanagh, a descendant of Dermot McMorrough, but the mother of his heir was May Etheridge, a former Gaiety chorus girl at the Shaftesbury Theatre in London. The Duke committed suicide in a Pimlico bed-sitter in 1975. Gerald, the 8th Duke of Leinster, who died at the age of ninety in December 2004, also lived in England. He had served with the Royal Inniskilling Dragoon Guards during the Second World War, and subsequently he was a partner in an aviation company in Oxford. The 9th Duke of Leinster, Maurice, owns a landscape gardening business in Oxfordshire. His son and heir, Thomas, Earl of Offaly died in a car accident in Cork in May 1997, and he had two daughters. The heir to the title is now Maurice's brother John, a racehorse trainer.

## Lord Walter, an Exceptional Gentleman

Lord Walter, the fourth son of the 4th Duke of Leinster, was born in 1858. Educated at Eton and Sandhurst he was gazetted to the 4th Battalion of the 60th Rifles in 1879, and after some years of service in India he retired as Captain in 1888, but he held a commission in the Carlow Militia for another decade. A story was later told about his relaxed military manner, such as when he was exercising troops on the rifle range, instead of giving the normal order *Fire* he always shouted *'Blaze away boys!'*

Lord Walter was present at the inaugural meeting of the County Kildare Archaeological Society at Palmerstown, the residence of the Earl of Mayo, in 1891 and was elected to the Council. Within a couple of years he was Honorary Secretary of the Society, an office that

*A rare photograph of Lord Walter*
*FitzGerald*

he held until his death. He enjoyed travelling around the county talking to old men, later recording their folk beliefs. One day he was talking to a farmer's daughter about a goat, and he asked her if they used the milk of the goat. She replied 'no, they kept the goat for luck, and they gave the kids away for the same reason. It would be unlucky to sell them.'

He contributed numerous papers to the Society's Journal, under his own name and under the pseudonym of *Omurethi*, and his final contribution was the note that *'Lord Edward's (FitzGerald) original Will, dated 27th May, 1798, is now in the possession of Lord Walter FitzGerald, who acquired it from the owner in May, 1920'*.

Lord Walter's final years were difficult. During the minority of his incapacitated nephew, the 6th Duke of Leinster, he was the trustee for the Leinster Estate, and had a big part in the negotiations for the sale of the property. He died at Kilkea Castle in July 1923, and his Obituary in the *Journal of the County Kildare Archaeological Society* described him as 'a unique personality, filled with a more genuine love of Ireland than the hackneyed word patriot can convey, he literally devoted the greater part of his life to scouring the whole south and west of this country, but especially his beloved Kildare, in search of antiquities.'

Lord Walter's grand-nephew, Edward, the 7th Duke, departed Kilkea in the 1960s, but the family graveyard there remains FitzGerald property.

The great FitzGerald house and estate at Carton, with its demesne walls, is still largely intact, but houses and two golf courses have been created, and the house is being developed as a hotel. Kilkea Castle has also been developed as such. Maynooth castle, the original FitzGerald stronghold, though a ruin, is preserved as a National Monument, and a portion of it has been restored for heritage purposes.

*Kilkea Castle, Francis Grose, The Antiquities of Ireland, 1794*

# 4

# Contrasting Origins

## *Sherlocks of Sherlockstown*

The arrival of the Anglo-Normans in Ireland in the last decades of the twelfth century heralded an infusion of new blood into the dominantly Gaelic population, and the creation of a new society. While the FitzGeralds were to become the lords of Kildare, other families also prospered here, such as those of Sherlock and Aylmer.

Having settled here by 1299, for over six hundred years the family of Sherlock was a prominent one in the County Kildare, and they gave their name to a town land. In the *County Kildare Exchequer Inquisition,* taken at Naas in 1551, Robert Sherlock of Sherlockstown was listed as a juror, and another branch of the family lived nearby at Little Rath, one of whom, Christopher Sherlock, was returned for the borough of Naas in 1613.

The Civil Survey of 1654-1656 records Sir John Sherlocke Knight, Protestant, of Little Rath, as the owner of 170 acres, which 'meareth on the East with ye lands of Sherlockestowne. There is one stone house with an orchard thereunto adjoining upon aforesaid lands of Little Rath. There is one Ash Parke upon aforesaid lands of Little Rath which is valued to be worth £30 sterling.' Christopher Sherlock of Daars, a Catholic and an officer in the army of the convert to Catholicism King James II, was attainted and his property forfeited. In 1691 the Commissioners of the Revenue let the property at a yearly rent to one Maurice Annesley, who became guardian to Philip Sherlock's younger children, and from time to time purchased from them or their representatives portions charged upon the estate. In 1705 one of the offspring, Eustace Sherlock, alleged that this purchase by Annesley was fraudulent, and laid claim to the portions which had been sold. Soon after Eustace Sherlock died, but his widow Hester Sherlock, a lady of remarkable determination, took out letters of administration and continued the suit. From that time on Annesley's life must have been an unhappy one. The suit was presented and seems to have gone against the lady, but in 1715 she appealed to the Irish House of Lords. Annesley met this 'with an appeal to the Lords' House in England, which mightily offended the Irish Peers, and on 23 September 1717 they resolved that no appeal lay to the English Lords, and that this House will support its honor, jurisdiction and privileges by giving Hester Sherlock effectual relief.'

Within ten days the Committee of the Irish Lords reported that £1,507 was due to Mrs Sherlock on account of principal and interest owing to one of the Sherlock brothers; and it was ordered that the Sheriff of Kildare should put her in possession until she was paid. This was done, and this very resolute lady proceeded at once to receive the rents, and make the most of her opportunity. But she neglected the estate and allowed it to fall into ruin, and pulled down the improvements Annesley had made. In fact her period of occupation ended in the decay of the old mansion and offices. Despite an appeal to the English

*Sherlockstown in 1911, from the Journal of the Kildare Archaeological Society, Vol. VI, 1911*

Lords, Annesley made no progress, and there was no authority willing to enforce the law. Feelings ran high, and for fear of arrest he left the country, as no Irish lawyer would take up his case.

That the William Sherlock of Sherlockstown in 1700 was a gentleman of some refinement is suggested by the contents of a letter written to him in March of that year by a Dublin wine merchant. He informed Sherlock that 'The wines and water are both lodged in the store waiting for you to send for them, the wine in a wretched case, having received great damage when the vessel put in at Dover...I have a few days ago accepted a Bill drawn upon me from Liége on your account for I think £31, English money, between £34 and £35 Irish money. I must request that you will enclose me a draft on Latouche for the whole, which with the freight may come to about £40.'

The 1752 Noble & Keenan map of Kildare, and Alexander Taylor's map of 1777, show Little Rath and Sherlockstown as small gentlemen's houses close to the road from Naas to Straffan. William Sherlock was a subscriber to Taylor & Skinner's *Maps of the Roads of Ireland,* also published in 1777. Sherlock, who was Ranger of the Curragh, is mentioned in the ballad *The Clane Rangers* as a member of *The Clane Rangers Volunteers* in 1779.

In 1814 William Sherlock was resident at *Sherlock's-town,* and some two decades later Sherlockstown House was listed in *Lewis's Topographical Directory* as 'the handsome modern mansion of W.R. Sherlock Esq., and *Prospect* belonging to the same family.' William R. Sherlock, in 1841, was committed to the Sheriff's Prison for debt. A report from the physician there in June of that year noted that Sherlock 'was now sober and under strict surveillance with two keepers in attendance...but when I went to the Prison last night, I found him grossly drunk, and had him removed to the Infirmary.' The misfortunes of the family continued with the natural deaths within a short time of William and his two brothers, Richard and Frank. Richard's son William, who was educated at Trinity College, became a Church of Ireland clergyman. Appointed Vicar of Clane in 1888, he was married to a Sherlock cousin, and they had four daughters. They lived at Sherlockstown, and were listed as the owners of 1,202 acres in the county. Sherlockstown is a long castellated house, with a tower, battlemented gables, turrets and a cloister. Griffith's *Valuation* of 1853 records some 860 acres as the property of Rep. William Sherlock. By then the town land of Little Rath, in the parish of Bodenstown, was owned by George Payne and occupied by Robert Hall.

*The Ven. William Sherlock, Archdeacon of Kildare*

In 1896 Canon William Sherlock of Sherlockstown was a Council Member of the *County Kildare Archaeological Society,* and he was later Hon. Editor for many years. Archdeacon of Kildare in 1909, he died a decade later, and Miss Sophie M. Sherlock succeeded him at Sherlockstown. With her demise yet another long established gentry family in the county came to an end. The estate was sold in 1953, and so ended the long tenancy of the Sherlock family in the County Kildare.

## Borrowes of Gilltown

The Borrowes family has been described as 'a scion of the ancient house of De Burgh, for centuries so eminent under the names of Burgh, Bourke, Burke, and Borough'. They were settled in Kildare since the sixteenth century, when the Elizabethan adventurer Henry Borrowes had married in succession Jane Savage of Rheban, Athy and Catherine Eustace of Gilltown, Kilcullen. Subsequently men of the family married into the noble houses of Kildare and Mayo, and into the lesser gentry families such as the Weldons of Athy, the Dixons of Calverstown, and the Higginsons of Mount Ophaley, Athy. A visitor to Rheban in September 1771 was Anne Cooke, later to be the wife of Walter Weldon M.P., who recorded in her diary 'my sister and I went to Athy in ye morning. Dine at Rheban. Sir Kildare Burros (5th Baronet) and Mr Higeson, of Mount Ophaley, and father of the then Lady Borrowes, dine with us.'

When the Curragh Commission was sitting in 1866 Major Sir Erasmus-Dixon Borrowes, who was vice-chairman of the Naas Board of Guardians, a member of the Board of Superintendents of Naas jail, and a member of the County Grand Jury, gave evidence on behalf of all three bodies. He was not enthusiastic with the occupation of the Curragh by the military, then in hutments, believing that it brought extra expense to the county through increases in the inmates of both the workhouse and the jail, and a curtailment of rights-of-way on the plain.

In 1897 the major saw his Victorian red brick mansion at Gilltown, less than forty years built, accidentally burned down; local lore is that the neighbours watched the mansion burn with little sympathy for Sir Erasmus, who was unpopular, as despite the nearness of the lake, enough water could not be drawn. That house had replaced an eighteenth century residence, the icehouse of which survives, as does the grandiose crested pyramid which marks the burial place of the Borrowes family at Gilltown. The other Borrowes' residence, Barretstown Castle, has been described by Mark Bence Jones as 'an old Eustace tower house with a two storey slightly Gothic Victorian addition.' The good relationship between the military and the county gentry was obvious in 1899 when the Hussars held their point-to-point at Barretstown, and the earl of Mayo, Lt Col. de Robeck, Col. Crichton, Sir Kildare Borrowes and Mr T. J. de Burgh were stewards.

The castle, in more recent years for a time having being occupied by the *parfumiere* Elizabeth Arden, was later presented to the nation by Mr W. G. Weston, the Canadian grocery billionaire, and today is home to the *Barretstown Gang Camp*.

## Aylmers of Donadea

The Aylmers have been recorded as 'one of the chief families of Anglo-Norman and early English settlers in County Kildare immediately after the English invasion.' They were established at Lyons by 1300, and if they did not achieve the status of the FitzGeralds, the Aylmers were also to become major landowners. By the year 1600 they were listed amongst the principal gentry in the county.

Over the centuries they held many positions of national or county importance, but in the seventeenth century, like many of the other landed Catholic families, they suffered. Their castles at Donadea and at Lyons were destroyed, and at Lyons Lady Ellen Aylmer, in the absence of her husband who was imprisoned in Dublin, defended her home against the army of her brother the Earl of Ormonde.

Men of the family were attainted and outlawed and, in Cromwellian times, deprived of their lands and transplanted. Aylmers joined the Wild Geese in the armies of Spain and France, in which countries also their womenfolk were to be found in convents. As was then customary, some of the family conformed to the established church, and so retained their properties.

The main residences of the family were at Lyons, the home of the senior branch until 1796, Donadea to 1935, and Courtown, which was sold in 1947. Courtown had been looted and burned during the Rebellion of 1798, when men of the family fought on both

*The remains of the medieval Donadea Castle were incorporated into the mansion which is now a ruin*

the government and rebel sides. It was rebuilt about 1815, and enlarged at the end of the nineteenth century.

In February 1789 *The Dublin Evening Post* reported that 'At the County Kildare Merry Harrier Clubroom, Clane, on Monday the 16 February, will be a Charity ball, under the patronage of Mrs Burdett, Mrs FitzGerald, Mrs Wolfe, Mrs Esmonde, Mrs Griffith, Mrs Browne and Mrs Aylmer, who will provide supper, etc.'

Mrs Esmonde was the wife of Dr John Esmonde, who came from a long established County Wexford family. He had married Helen O'Callan, co-heiress with her sisters of Bartholomew O'Callan of Osberstown, Sallins. Col. Dr John Esmonde is described in *Burke's Dictionary of the Peerage etc.* as having 'perished a victim to the political disturbance of 1798.' He was hanged as a rebel from Carlisle Bridge in Dublin on the 14 June 1798.

One of his brothers was a Jesuit, Fr Bartholomew, who for a time was Rector of Clongowes Wood College, and who died at St Francis Xavier's, Gardiner St, Dublin in 1862. Fr Bartholomew had combined with his neighbour and fellow Jesuit, Fr Charles Aylmer of Painstown, and Fr Paul Ferley, in the publication of *A Short Explanation of the Principle Articles of the Catholic Faith,* and *The Devout Christian Daily Companion.* James Esmonde, an uncle of the priest, lived at Sallins. His wife was Anne FitzGerald from nearby Yeomanstown.

Sir FitzGerald Aylmer, 7th Baronet of Donadea, was brought up as a Protestant, and Margaret, his only daughter, married Sir John Hort, Baronet of nearby Hortland, who was a son of the Protestant Archbishop of Tuam. Sir FitzGerald's eldest son and heir, Sir Fenton Aylmer, narrowly escaped death in 1798 when a rebel force led by his kinsman William Aylmer of the Roman Catholic, Painstown, Kilcock branch of the family, attacked his yeomanry unit. Having survived the rebellion, William Aylmer went to Austria and enlisted in the army where he went from the rank of vice-corporal to that of lieutenant and captain. By 1816 he was in London, instructing the Dragoons in the art of the sword, and from there he returned home to his brother's house at Painstown. After a few years he tired of rural life and decided to seek adventure in South America in the army of Simon Bolivar where he was appointed commander of the Irish Legion of the Revolutionary Army. He died from wounds received in battle in 1820.

*Sir Fenton Aylmer, a founder of the Kildare Hunt*

Charles Aylmer, a brother of the rebel leader, was educated on the continent, and ordained into the *Society of Jesus* in 1814. Three years later he was appointed Rector of Clongowes Wood. Superior of the Society's house in Gardiner St, Dublin when the foundation stone of the church of St Francis Xavier was laid, he inherited the Painstown property on the death of his brother Robert in 1841. He died in 1847. In 1807 T. J. Rawson, the improving farmer from Athy, had mentioned Sir Fenton Aylmer in his *Statistical Survey of the County Kildare*, as the owner of 'the conical hill of Allen....among the rocks is also found a stone, which from its texture would be proper for millstones. It has since proved to be the most valuable kind. Sir Fenton Aylmer holds out every encouragement for its being extensively worked: Some spirited adventurer may make a fortune'. How right he was! The quarrying there has indeed proved to be a fortune to the owners, and an important source of employment locally.

The Baronet was also credited with the establishment of the Kildare Hunt, of which he was Master in 1813 when a great misfortune befell the pack. The hunt had met at Tipper, near Naas, and they were moving towards Glending when, to quote the *Sporting Magazine*:

'from a small unenclosed scrub of hazel a large greyhound fox jumped up almost among the hounds. He proved a mountaineer from Wicklow, for disregarding the adjacent earth and coverts, he made straight for the Wicklow hills over such country and at such a pace as flung the whole field with the exception of two who, being on that day the best mounted, and having fortunately been riding in advance of the hounds, got such a start as enabled them to keep in sight. Indeed, though it was for Ireland open, the hills were so severe that nothing but blood could live through it, and one of these nags was thorough, the other better than three parts bred. He passed the Liffey head and without check gained the romantic rocks, plantation and waterfall of *Poul-a-Phouca* where the river Liffey is precipitated over a high and rugged ridge of rocks, and which was then unusually swollen by a succession of rainy weather. In this plantation on the other side of *Poul-a-Phouca* was the villain's den, and as it came in view, the hounds were close at his brush; a distance of 12 miles, all nearly against the hill, having been done in thirty-five minutes.'

'To reach the highland home he had to cross the river, and no other but the desperate alternative of passing over the fall, where being narrowly enclosed by rocks, it was diminished to the width of a wide brook. This he attempted and was swept down the fall with twelve couple and a half of the leading hounds, which had thrown themselves after him with the same headlong desperate resolution. When the huntsmen and the writer of this, who were the next up, arrived, they were all in one *mêlée,* fox and hounds, in foaming eddies under the fall; some were killed in the descent, others maimed but yet living, among whom was *Caitiff;* and some one or two almost exhausted reached land. When Grennon, the huntsman, saw the elite of his pack thus swept before his eyes, he stood, for assistance was impossible, for some time like a statue, but when he was assured by their lifeless remains floating in the pool below, the fall of the loss of two particular veterans, he could stand it no longer, but burst into tears, and wept long and bitterly.'

During the famine years of the nineteenth century the 15,396–acre Donadea estate benefited from extensive relief works, including the building of the demesne walls and the making of an ornamental lake. In wintertime the ice was taken from the lake and stored in the icehouse for use in the castle during the summer months.

On the death of Sir Justin Gerard Aylmer in 1885 his sister Caroline Maria Aylmer became the owner of the Estate, and her distant relative Alan Aylmer Luxmore sometimes came to stay. He recalled his first visit when 'Donadea was still carried on as a prosperous country house and estate and Miss Aylmer lived with two companions, Miss Light who was a daughter of Canon Light, prominent writer of hymns, and a Miss Mackenzie. There was an agent, Captain Maunsell (Land Agents were commonly called 'Captain'), who lived in a separate tower built by Sir Gerard Aylmer for his own use and fortified with cannon, which I was informed were only removed in 1966. Maunsell was a very useful chap! He arranged tennis parties and picnics to the tower of Allen, and whatever you wanted.'

Aylmer Luxmore also remembered being attended by servants in the castle, 'who were fairly numerous owing to the extra work of pumping up from the lake and carrying all the water for baths, etc. as there was too much lime in it to let it go through the pipes without corroding them. This also meant that everyone breakfasted in bed and had a hip-bath in their bedroom. The other meals were formal, and there was some entertaining and often a drive with two horses in the afternoon.'

Miss Aylmer was at that time farming on a large scale, with an out-farm at the Hill of Allen, beneath the viewing tower which had been built by an ancestor a century before. She won prizes for horse breeding, but also found time to paint and to exhibit her pictures in Dublin. When she died in 1935 she left the proceeds of the sale of her estate to the Church of Ireland, from whom the property passed into State ownership. It is now a forest park managed by *Coillte Teo*. In the church there, which is still in use, is the seventeenth century canopied altar tomb of Sir Gerald Aylmer and his wife Dame Julia Nugent.

Michael Aylmer of Courtown, Kilcock married in 1853 Charlotte Margaret Hendrick, daughter and heiress of Hans Hendrick of Kerdiffstown House, Naas, and his wife Marianne Borrowes, the eldest daughter of Sir Erasmus-Dixon Borrowes of Barretstown Castle, Ballymore Eustace. When she died in 1862 Hans Hendrick married her first cousin, Jane Harriette, daughter of Sir Kildare Borrowes. The second son of Michael Aylmer and Charlotte Hendrick was Hendrick Hendrick-Aylmer who assumed the surname Hendrick in 1889, two years after his grandfather Sir Erasmus-Dixon Borrowes, Major Borrowes of Gilltown, and T. Hendrick of Kerdiffstown were mentioned in the army's list of *Gentry & c. of the Neighbourhood*. Sir Kildare Borrowes of Gilltown was High Sheriff in 1902, and resident at Barretstown Castle, Ballymore Eustace.

Col. R. M. Aylmer, who served in both the First and Second World Wars, sold Kerdiffstown in 1938 (in 1883 the Kerdiffstown estate consisted of 3,088 acres) and moved to Ayesha Castle, County Dublin. He was a grandson of Michael Aylmer of Courtown. His aunt Florence, only daughter of Michael and Charlotte (Hendrick) Aylmer had married Lt. Col. W. J. Borrowes, son of Sir Erasmus Dixon Borrowes 8th Baronet.

Now there is none of the Aylmer families' resident in County Kildare, but there are representatives living in County Dublin, and the Canadian born 16th Baronet of Donadea has in recent years made frequent visits to Ireland, and was for a time a Council Member of the County Kildare Archaeological Society.

When the Aylmer family discovered in 1878 that their grave stones at Lyons had been levelled in 1799 they erected a plaque in the graveyard to record that fact, but Lord Cloncurry was not pleased and removed it. The Aylmers then had it erected in the ruined church at Johnstown Inn, but by 1901 it was again missing. Over sixty years later it was discovered in the basement of Palmerstown, where Lord Mayo must have stored it, and the County Kildare Archaeological Society then arranged to have it returned to Lyons.

The Aylmers were also connected to the Horts of Hortland House, some five miles southwest of Kilcock. Designed by Richard Castle for the Revd Josiah Hort, Archbishop of Tuam, who purchased Sullogestown, now Hortland, in 1748, it was a two storey five bay small mansion with a Venetian window over a pedimented doorway. In 1913 it was described as 'sadly dilapidated', and it is now demolished.

Archbishop Hort, the son of a Gloucestershire man, was educated at Cambridge and subsequently ordained to the Church of England. Appointed in 1709 as chaplain to the lord-lieutenant, he was soon the incumbent of a parish, and then dean of Cloyne and Ardagh. Subsequently he was bishop of Ferns and bishop of Kilmore, before being elevated to the See of Tuam in 1742. In the meantime he had married a sister of the first earl of Kerry. They had a family of three sons and four daughters.

His son John, who held the position of British consul-general at Lisbon during the Peninsular War, succeeded the prelate at Hortland. His correspondence from there includes references to the arranged marriages of the Portuguese royal family: 'marriage of the infanta, aged thirty, to her nephew, the prince of Beira, aged fifteen,' and in 1784: 'marriage announced between the second prince of Portugal aged seventeen, and the infanta of Asturia aged nearly nine.' When he returned to Kildare the consul himself married into the county gentry in the person of Margaret, a daughter of Sir FitzGerald Aylmer of Donadea.

During the 1798 Rising Hortland was damaged by the rebels, and in the *List of Suffering Loyalists* is a claim from Sir John Hort for compensation of £950.12.9, for general loss at Hortland. Sir John and Lady Margaret had, in due course, a large family, and eventually Hortland passed to the eldest son, Sir Josiah William the 2nd Baronet, High Sheriff and Member of Parliament for Kildare. His heir, Sir John, served in the Crimean war, and as he was unmarried his brother Sir William FitzMaurice Hort succeeded. Though twice married, Sir William died without an heir and the baronetcy passed to a younger brother, Sir Fenton Joshua. He was an officer in the Inniskilling Fusiliers, and lived at Hortland, but did not marry. The title then went to a junior branch of the family. Hortland was sold to the tenants early in the twentieth century.

In 1882 the Hort estate had consisted of 3,956 acres in Kildare, Queen's county and Fermanagh. Of the Hort women one is remembered as a famous beauty. She was Frances, the second daughter of the founding father, the archbishop of Tuam. Married to Lord Boringdon, she was painted by Angelica Kauffmann in the character of a muse of poetry crowning the poet Ossian. This acrostic on her name was published in *Exshaw's Magazine* in 1758:

F air! beyond expression fair!
R osy lips and auburn hair,
A labaster neck and breast,
N ature's masterpiece confessed;
C heerful azure of the skies
E ver blooming in her eyes:

S uch the lovely nymph I prize.
H appy he who shall receive her;
O h! the wretch condemned to leave her;
R ather 'tis a curse than blessing
T hus to see without possessing.

## Wogans of Rathcoffey

A relationship between the neighbouring and long established Roman Catholic families of Aylmer and Wogan had been formed in the early seventeenth century when Matthew Aylmer from Ballycanon married Elizabeth Wogan of Rathcoffey. One distinguished member of that family was Sir Charles Wogan who participated in a venture which was to be immortalised in fact and in fiction.

The following quotation, from A.E.W. Mason's novel *Clementina* published in 1926, gives the names of the four gentlemen from County Kildare who in 1719 successfully undertook to bring the Princess Sobieski from Austria to Italy where she was to marry James III, the Old Pretender: 'Misset started up from his chair and leaned forward. 'The king,' said O'Toole, 'to be sure, that makes a difference.' Gaydon asked quietly: 'And what is the prize?' 'The Princess Clementina,' said Wogan, 'We are to rescue her from her prison in Innsbruck.'

All of the men were officers in the Irish regiment of Dillon, serving in France, and the leader of the group was Charles Wogan. All four were said to be kinsmen: Capt. John Misset was from Dowdenstown, Major Richard Gaydon from Irishtown, but the home of O'Toole is not known.

Sir Charles Wogan was from the branch of the family settled in county Kildare since the early fourteenth century, and which had intermarried with other old county families such as the FitzGeralds, Eustaces, Aylmers, and the Brownes of Clongowes Wood. As well as penning his narrative of the Innsbruck expedition in French, Wogan wrote poetry and prose in Latin and English. In 1732 he had sent a cask of wine to Dean Jonathan Swift, with a collection of writings in a green velvet bag, hoping that the dean could have them published. James Ward, a student at Clongowes in 1988, commenting on that transaction said: 'Swift drank the wine, but the writings remained unpublished.'

An earlier generous gesture by a lady of the family was also unappreciated. In the troubled year of 1641 Mary Wogan of Rathcoffey, the ninety-year old wife of James Eustace of

THE WOGAN ARMS.

*The Wogan Arms*

Clongowes, received the Puritan commander Captain Hues at Clongowes and 'entertained him friendly.' His appreciation of the hospitality was to hang the lady, 'and to convey the soldiers to Dublin, and hanged them there; upwards of 150 women and children found in the same place (Clongowes) were murdered, including Eustace.' Another version of this story which names Francis More from County Louth as the perpetrator of that atrocious crime is told in the next chapter.

John Browne, a Dublin barrister, whose father was believed to have lived at Jigginstown, Naas, was granted the forfeited estates of the Eustaces of Clongowes Wood by Charles II in 1667, on the payment of a mortgage of £2,100. But, before that, the castle there had been blown up 'to make it uninhabitable for the rebels,' and it was not until the second decade of the eighteenth century that Stephen William Browne, a grandson of the grantee, restored the castle as a residence. He also sought to erect a monument and to restore his family's burial place within the old parochial church at Mainham, but when the parson asked for the sum of £5 for the permit, Browne refused to pay. Instead he built a mausoleum outside the boundary of the churchyard, and put up a plaque outlining his dispute with the parson. Then he also had the bones of some his ancestors removed from St Audeon's in Dublin for burial at Mainham. The mausoleum is now in the care of Kildare County Council.

Stephen Browne had married into the neighbouring Catholic family of Wogan from Rathcoffey, and his son Michael, a colonel in the French army, also married a girl of the Wogans. Another son, Anthony, was a colonel in the army of the King of Saxony. Early in the eighteenth century two members of the family were included in the list of *Persons of Popish religion within the Kingdom of Ireland* who were licensed to bear arms; each of them 'might carry one sword, one case of pistols, and one gun'.

Men of the Browne family also served with distinction in European armies, one of whom reached the rank of Marshal in the Austrian service, and was killed at the battle of Prague in 1757. It was believed that his sisters, at home in Clongowes, were alarmed one day when some of the servants said they had seen an officer in uniform, with his hands to his breast which was bleeding, coming to the hall door. The ladies assumed that the apparition was a warning of their brother's death. Mourning was commenced, masses celebrated

*The Mausoleum of the Brown family at Mainham*

*Clongowes Wood College c1900. Thomas Wogan Brown built the gothic revival castle in 1788, and it was sold to The Society of Jesus in 1814, and it is still a College*

and a wake held. A couple of weeks later a dispatch came announcing the marshal's death on the day on which the apparition had been seen!

Another General, Michael Browne of the Saxony army, served under Napoleon before Moscow. The older brother of the General, Thomas Browne of Clongowes Wood, High Sheriff of the county, apostatized about 1772. A story told about him was that of his involvement in a curious incident one Sunday afternoon in 1797. As he was riding past a field where a football game was about to commence he was invited to give the kick-off 'a sort of friendly sanctioning of the amusements of the neighbours, which was then not unusual among the gentry,' as Lord Cloncurry later remarked. But when the Lord Chancellor learnt about Magistrate Browne's treasonable football he had him removed from the commission of the peace.

Browne's last public appearance was at a meeting of Protestant gentry at Naas in September 1811. It was later noted that then, 'though an apostate, he was a declared supporter of Catholic Emancipation. He affirmed that Catholic Emancipation was a Right, not a concession to be pleaded for, and that it should be unconditional too. He pointed out that his brother Michael could not live in the country as a gentleman of good position, unless Emancipation was affected.'

Margaret Gibbons in her book *Glimpses of Catholic Ireland in the 18th Century* wrote 'there was always hope that Thomas Browne would repent his apostasy; but he died in 1812, to all appearances as he lived.' Then his neighbours disputed as to whether he should be buried according to Catholic or Protestant rites; while he was accepted to have been of the latter persuasion, his brother and sister were Catholics. The quarrel continued over the coffin in the graveyard. Commenting on the affair Lord Cloncurry said 'No man ever was buried who during his life exhibited or entertained less of sectarian rancor, or whose living feelings were less in unison with the passions which signalized his funeral. He was a man of extremely amiable disposition, and filled with the most ardent love of his country, and the utmost desire to do his duty in all the relations of life.'

Browne's sister Judith had been educated at the Benedictine Convent at Ypres, where two of their aunts were nuns. Gibbons observed 'that after her brother's perversion, and not liking the gay life led by her brother and cousins, she took a house in Tullow close to the newly established convent of the *Daughter's of St Brigid*, and placed herself under the direction of Dr Daniel Delany, a future bishop of Kildare & Leighlin.'

Miss Browne, 'with her gracious and foreign culture, moved in at the bishop's request, and formed one of the conventual household, though she never took, as did the others, the three religious vows. She was there as a guide in religious routine, and as the teacher in the secular branches of the infant congregations.' When Bishop Delany died in 1814 he willed his property, including books, plate and pictures, 'to my esteemed friend Miss Judith Browne, actually residing in Tullow, and late of Castle Browne in County Kildare.'

Lt. General Michael Browne of Saxony sold the family seat at Clongowes Wood to the Jesuits in 1813, and so severed the link which had existed for two hundred years between his family and County Kildare. However, in the second half of the nineteenth century, the general's heir bought land and built a house near Naas, naming it *Keredern* after his wife, a daughter of General Baron de Keredern de Trobriand of the French army. His son, Col. Francis Wogan-Browne, adopted the additional surname of Wogan, to perpetuate the memory of that ancient Kildare family into which the Brownes had married.

Col. Wogan-Browne, who had served for twenty-seven years in the King's Own Hussars, took an active interest in the life of the county. He was a Justice of the Peace, a member of Naas Urban District Council, and of the *County Kildare Archaeological Society*. His only son, John, aged twenty-three in 1922, was serving as a lieutenant with the Royal Field Artillery in Kildare barracks. He maintained the family tradition of loyalty to the Catholic Church and was a daily Mass-goer. A keen rugby player, he was on the army team, and he also played for Lansdowne.

February 1922 was a time of high tension throughout the country. Dáil Éireann had just approved the Treaty which ended the Anglo-Irish war, and the withdrawal of British troops commenced, causing mixed feelings amongst many people. On the morning of Friday, 10 February 1922 Lt Wogan- Browne walked, as was his custom each week, to the Hibernian Bank in Kildare to collect the regimental pay. As he returned to barracks, at the junction of Infirmary Road, and not far from the back gate of the barracks, a car pulled up beside him and one of the three occupants grabbed the pay satchel. When Wogan-Browne made a dash to try and recover the bag one of the robbers shot him in the forehead. A soldier from the barrack gate ran to help the injured officer, while the robbers drove off in the car.

The murder of Wogan-Browne caused wide-spread horror throughout the county. The Requiem Mass in the Curragh Garrison Church, and the funeral to St Corban's Cemetery, Naas, were attended by huge crowds, including representatives of the IRA. The match at Lansdowne Road in which he was to have played was abandoned. General Michael Collins ordered that every effort should be made to capture the culprits, and the military police were joined in the search by the IRA (who claimed the assassins were not members). Alarmed by the murder and other outrages, Winston Churchill, the Secretary of State for the War Department, halted the withdrawal of the troops from Ireland, but within a few days Collins sent him a telegram saying he had 'just been notified by phone we have captured three of those responsible for the attack on Lt Wogan-Browne. Everyone, civilian and soldier, had co-operated in tracking those responsible for this abominable action. You may rely on it that those whom we can prove guilty will be suitably dealt with.' The three suspects were held in the barracks at Trim.

At the inquest into the killing, which was sat at the Curragh Military Hospital, it was established that the men had hired the Ford car and driver in Kildare for 15/-, purportedly for the conveyance of a patient to the Infirmary. Tom Graham, the driver, said that he did not know any of the men, and that he was forced to drive away from the scene of the crime with one of the men holding a revolver to his head. At Kildoon the men left the car and ran away. The entire incident of the shooting had taken just two minutes, and the sum procured was £135. At the end of the proceedings the coroner, Jeremiah O'Neill, said Wogan-Browne was from a distinguished family, and he asked the jury to express their sympathy on what he considered to be 'a most un-Irish incident,' adding 'it was the duty of the loyal people to join the Provisional Government in bringing the culprits to justice.'

In Kildare town rumours about the murder were widespread, and local Doctor L. F. Rowan wrote to the *Kildare Observer* to scotch one story: acknowledging that there had been hostile demonstrations by the military in the town on the night of the murder, and that traders' passes for access to the barracks had been stopped (thus putting their livelihood in danger), Rowan said that 'it was quite untrue that civilian witnesses to the murder scoffed at the dying officer.'

Following the loss of his son Col. Wogan-Browne sold *Keredern* and left Ireland, never to return. Five years later he died in France and was buried there. The three suspects of the crime were later released, and it was said that two of them joined the National Army.

But the family was not entirely forgotten, and on St Valentine's Day 1954 the *Wogan Society* held a Wogan Family Commemoration at Malahide Castle, Dublin. The venue was chosen, as the Talbot de Malahide family were the heirs of the Rathcoffey Wogans. Votes of thanks were given by General Sir Eric de Burgh, President of the *County Kildare Archaeological Society*, and by Revd Fr Finegan S.J. A lengthy report on the occasion in *The Irish Tatler & Sketch* concluded: 'The Jesuit Fathers of Clongowes are the legal heirs by purchase of the Wogan and Wogan-Brownes of Mainham and Castle Browne.'

## Eustaces of Harristown

From the fifteenth to the beginning of the eighteenth century the Eustaces were amongst the great landowners of the county, and they occupied many important positions, including that of Lord Chancellor. Maurice Eustace, who inherited Harristown in 1665, greatly embellished the estate, including the creation of an artificial lake, with floating on it a miniature man-o-war, equipped with real guns! Benefactors of the church, they produced ardent defenders of the old faith, as well as conformists to the new.

While the Eustace family of Castlemartin might claim to be the eldest of the line, it was from the Harristown branch, which was originally part of the Castlemartin estate, from which Lord Portlester and the viscounts Baltinglass hailed. They included Lt Gen. Charles Eustace of Robertstown who saw active service in the American War of Independence, and in 1798 he was present at the battle of Ross. He died in 1800 at the age of seventy-three, 'as a result of the hardships suffered during the fighting of 1798, having had eleven children,' according to the family historian, Major-General Sir Eustace F. Tickell, writing in the *Journal of the County Kildare Archaeological Society*.

Fr John Chetwode Eustace, born around 1762, and who died in 1815, was educated at Douai, and a priest of the diocese of Kildare & Leighlin. He was Professor of Rhetoric in Maynooth from 1795 to 1797. The former importance of the Eustace family in the Pale is recalled in the name of a village on the Liffey in County Kildare, Ballymore Eustace, the great town of the Eustaces, where Thomas Fitz Oliver Eustace was appointed constable in 1373.

ALLYMORE EUSTACE Caſtle, Co: of Wicklow. 16 ᴹ. from *Dublin*

*Delᵗ 1773.*

Ballymore Eustace Castle by Gabriel Beranger, 1773

Punchestown: Autotype made by J. O'Hea from Chancellor's stereo-photographs taken on the occasion of the visit of the Prince of Wales in 1869

Lady Pamela FitzGerald, wife of Lord Edward FitzGerald

*Opposite:*
*Top:* Arrest of Lord Edward Fitzgerald

*Bottom:* The Installation Banquet of the Knights of St. Patrick in St Patrick's Hall, Dublin Castle, 17 March 1783. An oil sketch by J K Sherwin. The group includes William Robert 2nd Duke of Leinster and Charles 6th Earl of Drogheda

The vault of the 17th century Jigginstown House, Naas built by Thomas Wentworth, Earl of Strafford

*Oppossite:*
*Top:* Rathcoffey Castle, the ruinous house of the Wogan Family

*Bottom:* Morristown Lattin from an 18th century engraving

Castletown House Celbridge, built from 1722 by Speaker Conolly

William Conolly, speaker of the Irish House of Commons 1715-1759, portrait dated 1727

Lady Anne Conolly, wife of Speaker William Conolly

Lady Louisa Conolly (1743–1821)

The print room at Castletown,
created by Lady Louisa
Conolly and her sister Lady
Sarah Napier about 1775

Castletown House aerial view

*Above:* Bishopscourt
House, built by Rt.
Hon John Ponsonby,
Speaker of the Irish
House of Commons,
1780

*Left:* Maria La Touche
1854

David La Touche in a portrait dated 1746

Lyons House, built by Nicholas Lawless, 1st Lord Cloncurry in 1797

Above left: *Sir Maurice Eustace, Lord Chancellor of Ireland*

Above right: *Lady Clotilda Eustace (1677-1737), who was the second wife of Sir Maurice Eustace of Harristown*

## Lattin, Mansfield & Sweetman families

The Mansfields of Morristown Lattin, Newbridge, for two hundred years one of the most prominent of the Roman Catholic gentry families in the county, originated in County Waterford. In 1722 John Mansfield married Jane Eustace of Yeomanstown, Naas, and by 1783 the Mansfields were in possession of the Eustace property. Again from inter-marriage, with the Lattin family of Morristown Lattin, they had inherited the Lattin property by 1817, and thus became major landholders in the county, with 4,542 acres in 1883.

The Lattin family is remembered at Naas in the Alms House for poor women, which they founded in 1590, and though thrice re-built, continues to fulfil its function. Almost two centuries after that benefaction a lady of the family merited mention in the *Dublin Magazine*. Mrs Lattin, who died aged ninety in 1764, was lauded as a 'mother, grand-mother, and great-grandmother to 87 children, all now living.' In fact, they were not all living. Her eldest son John had died at the age of twenty-one in 1731. Popularly called Jack Lattin he is remembered in the rhyme:

> Jack Lattin dressed in satin
> Broke his heart dancing:
> He danced from Castle Browne
> To Morristown.

Lattin is also commemorated in the tune *Jack Lattin that,* a couple of years after his death, was played on the pipes at a musical performance in Dublin.

Her next son, George, married Catherine, the daughter of Ambrose O'Ferrall of Balyna, Moyvalley, and their son Patrick, despite the fecundity of his grandmother, was the last

*George Mansfield, president of the
Kildare Archaeological Society, 1926*

male of the Morristown Lattins. He was educated in Paris and Turin before enlisting in the Irish Brigade.

Lady Morgan, the novelist whose salon was a centre of social and literary life in Kildare Street, Dublin, met Patrick Lattin when she was staying with the Cloncurry's at Lyons in 1827. He was on his annual holiday from Paris, and he brought Lady Morgan to visit Morristown Lattin in his old fashioned French coach. When in Paris a couple of years later she visited *Chaussée d'Antin* where her host was Patrick Lattin. She later recalled: 'That house where it is always such a privilege to dine; where the wit of the host, like the *menus* of his table, combines all that is best in French or Irish peculiarity.'

Patrick Lattin's daughter and heiress married Alexander Mansfield of Yeomanstown, Naas. Their 5th son, Edmund, a Major in the county Dublin Militia, was a member of the *Commission of Inquiry (into the matter of the Curragh of Kildare)*, which sat at the Court House in Newbridge in September 1866. He was well aware of the problem created in the neighbourhood of the Curragh by the *Wrens*, as the prostitutes who followed the troops were known. He described the women as 'The greatest public scandal, and the greatest indecency,' and agreed that the police should remove the women. In 1887 George Patrick Lattin Mansfield, an elder brother of the major's, was listed in the military *Official Directory to the County Kildare*, which served as a social guide for the officers.

George Mansfield had welcomed the Holy Family Sisters when they came to Newbridge from England in 1875, at the invitation of the Parish Priest to open a convent and school. Máire Ryan, in her book *The Holy Family in Newbridge*, notes that Mansfield was later referred to in the Order's journal as 'the richest Catholic proprietor in the County Kildare. He had provided the site for the Parish Church and parochial house in the 1840s, and it was on the same site that the convent was built. Mansfield advised the

The following Notice has been posted on all the bills of Battersby's Auction at Barretstown, Clongory on Tuesday and Wednesday next.

# COME AND SEE! COME AND SEE!

Great Sale by the celebrated Auctioner, Battersby, on Tuesday and Wednesday Next, Oct. 28th and 29th at

## BARRETSTOWN HOUSE, CLONGOREY

With the kind permission of "Dove" Grabber, Routledge Agent to the House Burner, Matty Maher, Ballinkeale, Enniscorthy, All That and Those the Embers and Ashes of the ruined & burned Homes of the Evicted Tenants.

Sale to commence sharp on the arrival of the Battering - Ram, Woods, &c.

*Anti-Eviction notice*

nuns on the lay-out of the convent grounds, and invited the Revd Mother to Morristown Lattin to see how his handsome place was laid out. This she duly did, accompanied by Sr Gertrude. They were received very graciously by Miss Mansfield and Miss Eustace and they walked through the pleasure grounds and garden.'

Mansfield continued to be a major benefactor of the parish and, in recognition of his generosity, it became a tradition in Newbridge that a man of the family would be one of the bearers who carried the canopy during the annual procession of the Blessed Sacrament at Corpus Christi; this practice lasted into the 1950s.

In the 1880s George Mansfield, as a trustee of the estate of the neighbouring, non-resident, Catholic O'Kelly family, had to cope with a very difficult agrarian situation. Due to exceptionally bad weather, and despite rent reductions, the tenants of the O'Kelly's at Clongorey were unable to pay their rents.

The fractious atmosphere and the subsequent evictions were very distressing for Mansfield, who was not in good health, and he died aged sixty-eight in 1889. His only son, George, was a founder member and first president of Naas Golf Club in 1896, and other gentry members included Mrs Hans Hendrick Aylmer of Kerdiffstown and Col. Wogan Browne from Keredern. Men of the Mansfield family married into that of the More-O'Ferrall's of Balyna, Moyvalley, (with whom there was already an old connection through the Lattins), and into the Sweetman family of Longtown, Clane. The status of those families is evident from the fact that when King George and Queen Mary visited Maynooth in 1911 members of them all were amongst the invitees to the college.

Michael Sweetman, from a Dublin brewing family, was living at Longtown late in the eighteenth century. His descendants filled the offices of High Sheriff and Justices of the Peace, and his great-grandson Gerard was a Member of Kildare County Council and

a Fine Gael TD for the county. Minister for Finance in the second Coalition government (1954-1957), he informed the senior steward of the Turf Club, Major Dermot
McCalmont, that it was perceived that 'the present members of the Turf Club were, for the
most part, out of touch with Irish affairs and were not representative of those interested
in and connected with the sport. Racing was no longer a rich man's sport, but becoming
more democratic every day. It was the shop window of an important national industry and
it was from that angle that he had to consider the matter. Questions might be asked in the
Dáil which he might find difficult to answer, and which might do infinite harm to racing
and everything connected with it.'

On that encounter the historian of the Turf Club, Fergus D'Arcy, commented: 'Genuine
solicitude or veiled threat aside, it is difficult to imagine a Minister for Finance, during one
of the worst periods in the economic history of the State, having so little to do as to worry
himself voluntarily about the composition of the governing body of a sport.'

Gerard Sweetman, who died in a motor accident in 1970, was married to Rosalind
Mansfield of Morristown Lattin. She was a celebrated beauty, and appeared in a series
of advertisements for the cosmetic *Ponds Cream,* featuring society ladies. Local rumour
at the time of her husband's entry into politics was that she commented: 'He had gone
native.'

Several women of the Sweetman family became nuns, including Margaret who, in the
late nineteenth century, was Superioress of the Sisters of Charity at Stanhope Street in
Dublin, while in 1945 Michael Joseph, who was educated at Clongowes, was ordained a
Jesuit priest.

A considerable archive of the *Mansfield Papers* was published in *Analecta Hibernica* in
1958, and in recent years the *Mansfield Papers,* described as 'a rich repository of materials
relating to the history of the Catholic landed gentry as well as the history of Irish landed
estates,' have been acquired by the National Library. Included in the *Papers* is the correspondence and writings of Patrick Lattin, as well as material concerning the management
of the estate in the nineteenth century.

## More O'Ferralls of Balyna

Callough O'More of Leix had been granted Balyna in 1574. His son, Col. Rory O'More,
was a leader of the Confederate Catholics in 1641, and his son, Col. Charles, raised a regiment of foot in the army of King James II. He was outlawed in 1688, and died in the Battle
of Aughrim in 1691. There was a legend that Rory had plunged his staff into the ground in a
wood, which until some years ago, existed at the back of Balyna house, and that it took root
and grew into a conifer. It was said that when the tree died the O'Mores or their descendants would cease to own Balyna. About 1957, when it was in poor condition, the tree fell in
a storm, and a few years later the property was sold by Gerald More O'Ferrall.

Rory's eldest daughter, Anne, was the wife of Patrick Sarsfield of Lucan, and their son
was created Earl of Lucan in 1690. As did many Catholic families in the Penal times, the
O'Ferralls sought careers on the continent, and men of the family reached the highest
ranks in the armies of Spain, and others were priests. One son was a Hereditary Roman
Senator, a General in the Spanish army and Governor of Barcelona. Some of the O'Ferrall
ladies entered convents, and one of them was a Maid of Honour to the Queen of Spain.
Women of the family married into the families of the O'Neill of the Fews, the Plunketts
of Meath, and the neighbouring Wogans of Rathcoffey. Other distinguished men of the
family were Ambrose O'Ferrall of Balyna who entered the Royal Sardinian service as a
Cornet of Dragoons, and retired as Major of Horse & Dragoons in 1790.

In the mid eighteenth century when Letitia More, an only child, inherited Balyna her marriage to Richard Ferrall created a new dynasty. It included The Rt. Hon. Richard More O'Ferrall, who was Lord of the Treasury, Secretary to the Admiralty and Secretary to the Treasury, and finally, Governor of Malta from 1847 to 1851.

In 1856 Charles Edward More O'Ferrall, a son of Maj. Ambrose More O'Ferrall, and who was educated at Clongowes, was High Sheriff of County Kildare. He married Susan O'Reilly, a descendant of a prosperous Dublin merchant family which had purchased the ancient FitzGerald castle at Kildangan. But as it was not a comfortable dwelling, and in 1748 the O'Reilly's had moved out, and into a single-storey thatched house, which was burned in 1880. Then More O'Ferrall had the castle demolished, and a house built in the Jacobean style.

About the same time, in 1885, when the Prince and Princess of Wales came to Punchestown, the Kildare Hunt Stewards, including Ambrose More O'Ferrall, with Percy La Touche and the young Earl of Mayo, and led by Lord Drogheda, greeted the royal couple. They witnessed the excitement of the Kildare Hunt Cup when the favourite *Nancy*, owned by the Baron de Robeck and ridden by his son Henry, slipped and fell at the first fence; but the rider remounted and went on to win!

The More O'Ferrall family had moved to this county following the murder of Richard More at their home, Lisard House, Edgeworthstown in 1935. His father was land agent for the former Edgeworth estate when the tenants disputed claims for rent. During a dinner party at Lisard four men forced their way into the house, and in the subsequent melee, both Gerald and his son wee shot, but by the time medical assistance arrived Richard had died. The attackers were arrested and charged, and found not guilty; on their return home they were greeted by a torch light procession and marching bands. Subsequently the O'Ferrall family left Edgeworthstown and moved to Kildare. Lisard was demolished in the 1950s, and the lands sold to the Forestry Department.

Roderick More O'Ferrall of Kildangan was a President of the Irish Bloodstock Breeder's Association, and a member of Kildare County Council. He had a major racing success in 1950 when his *Dark Warrior* won the Irish Derby. A prominent member of the Racehorse Owners Association, he had been an advocate of reforms in the sport, but it was to be several decades before major reforms were introduced.

Roderick's brother, Francis, was Chairman of the Anglo-Irish Bloodstock Agency in London, and their youngest brother, Edward Roger Mary Joseph, was Chairman of More O'Ferrall Ltd. He was married to Lady Elizabeth Cecilia, a daughter of the Earl of Listowel, and the widow of Viscount Elveden.

## Archbolds of Timolin

The Archbold family, of Danish descent, was settled in Timolin by 1590, in which year Walter Archbold was granted a twenty-one year lease of lands by the earl of Kildare. Described as 'titular Barons of Timolin,' they intermarried with their fellow county families of Eustace and Sherlock. At Moone Abbey the altar-tomb of Walter Archbold and his wives, Elizabeth Eustace and Anne Usher, dated 1629, recently has been restored by *Dúchas*. Staunchly Catholic, in 1661 Christopher Archbold of Timolin signed the *Remonstrance of the Roman Catholic Nobility and Gentry*, acknowledging Charles II as lawful king.

In 1747 the Archbolds had the dubious distinction of being visited by the notorious highwayman Capt. James Freney, who had discovered that Mr Archbold had 'a fine house and a good deal of money and plate.' Locally he learnt that Archbold was 'a jolly well looking little man which denoted his having something considerable in his house.'

The captain and his men decided to call on the Archbolds. Breaking their way into the house through a window, one of the intruders confined the men servants in their bedroom while Freney went to the Archbold bedroom where he found the lady of the house, and learned that the master (William Archbold was High Sheriff of Kildare in the 1740s) was away from home. Though Freney told the woman that she should not be frightened she was naturally alarmed by his companions, who had their faces blackened. Freney ordered her to get dressed and to show them the house, but she pleaded that she was too terrified and that her cousin who was upstairs would guide them. After some calming words from Freney, Mrs Archbold handed over the keys of her desk. When the robbers had collected £400 in plate and cash they left the house and went to find their horses, only to discover that the animals had strayed and could not be found in the dark. Eventually a horse was procured to carry the plate, and the thieves set off for Kilkenny. No further mention of the escapade has been found.

At the end of the eighteenth century James Archbold married Eleanor Kavanagh of Borris, and their daughter married into the Cassidys, the Monasterevan distillers. Davidstown, Castledermot, the Archbolds' fine eighteenth century house on 3,000 acres, passed in 1877 from Robert Archbold, High Sheriff of the county, to his sister Mary. Their mother was Mary Power from Faithlegg, County Waterford, and about thirty years ago the estate came by descent to the present owner Gerald Gallwey (whose mother was also a Power), and who had served in the Irish Guards in the Second World War. Davidstown is one of the oldest houses of a gentry family in County Kildare to be still occupied by a descendant of the original owners. But there are now only a few representatives of any of the old Roman Catholic families living in the county of Kildare.

# 5

# Three Peers

*Bourkes of Palmerstown*

In the late decades of the eighteenth century three titled families resident in County Kildare were advanced in the peerage: John Bourke, Viscount Mayo of Palmerstown, was created Earl of Mayo, while the Earl of Drogheda, Monasterevan, was advanced to the rank of Marquis in 1791. John Stratford of Belan had become Earl of Aldborough in 1777.

If the Bourke family of Palmerstown, Johnstown, Naas, could, like the FitzGeralds, claim descent from the first Norman settlers, they did not settle in County Kildare until the middle of the seventeenth century. By the mid-nineteenth century they held over 1000 acres at Johnstown, and with their distant kinsmen the Burghs of Oldtown, Naas, they also became major land owners in the town, and for decades controlled the Corporation and the office of Sovereign. The family gave many sons to the church and the army, and in 1785 they had received the title of Earl of Mayo. Commenting on that elevation, Michael Davitt described John Bourke as 'a successful place-man, owner of a nomination borough, was made Lord Naas, and afterwards created a peer as Earl of Mayo. The customary £15,000 compensation followed the title as the price of the borough.'

In the graveyard at Johnstown is the monument to commemorate the 6th Earl of Mayo who, as Viceroy of India, was assassinated in 1872. His home was Palmerstown, and he was a descendant of John Bourke, captain of horse, and his wife Catherine Fay, who lived at Kill from about 1641. This family of Bourke was known as the Mac William Bourkes, and they claimed as ancestor William Fitzadelm de Burgo, who had succeeded Strongbow as governor of Ireland in 1177.

*John Burke, 1st Earl of Mayo*

Theobald was the first of them to settle at Palmerstown. He was Member of Parliament for Naas, and he died in 1726 to be succeeded by his nephew John. He was within a few years to become involved in an unseemly row with another county gentleman, Alexander Graydon of Killashee, in contesting the office of Town Sovereign. Bourke was a member of the Privy Council, and his wife was a daughter of the Lord Chief Baron of the Exchequer. In 1767 he was MP for Naas, and in the following years both he and his son held that seat; he was also Sovereign of Naas in 1769, and again in 1771 and 1774. Elevated to the peerage as Baron of Naas in 1776, he was advanced to Viscount Mayo, and created Earl of Mayo in 1785.

In 1767 the vestry of St David's church in Naas agreed that the ruinous church steeple should be pulled down and another built 'in such place in the churchyard as should be approved by John Bourke, one of the Commissioners of H. M. Revenue. It was to be built after the manner of St Patrick's, Dublin, sufficient to contain a ring of eight bells of equal size with the bells of St Patrick's steeple, and they grant to John Bourke and his heirs £100 per annum for thirty-one years out of the revenue of the Corporation for the said purpose. Any residue to be spent repairing and adorning the church.' The building of the steeple commenced in 1780, and two years later it had reached the second floor, but eventually the tower was never completed.

John Bourke's eldest son, the 2nd Earl who had married a daughter of the Earl of Milltown from Russborough, died without issue, so a younger son, who was Archbishop of Tuam, became the third Earl.

An officer who was stationed at Naas Barracks in 1832 wrote in his diary 'I only know two families in the neighbourhood, Lord Mayo's and Major Tandy's the Stipendiary Magistrate, the latter I have the pleasure of seeing too frequently as I am continually accompanying him to the Tithe Sales, Tithe Meetings etc. a very harassing and disagreeable duty for the Military. He is always very civil inviting me invariably to dinner, I have only dined twice there, and then I had to complain of being very crowded at table, a common occurrence in this country, for they think nothing of making twenty people sit down when there is only room for sixteen. At Palmerstown they live in a very good style, an excellent cuisine and if I mistake not a French artiste.'

The following year Robert Bourke was Sovereign (Mayor) of Naas, and a report of the commissioners appointed to investigate the Corporation of Naas in that year found it to be 'most unpopular, and as at present constituted does not exist for any useful purpose. A glance at the roll of officer holders for the previous thirty years showed that only twice in that time had persons other than members of the Bourke family been Sovereign.' Commenting that the purpose of the corporation was 'that all of the inhabitants and their successors should be members of it, it was now composed entirely of members of Lord Mayo's family, as twelve of them (or his tenants or agents) filled the fifteen positions of burgesses and freemen. There was no instance of a Roman Catholic or Protestant Dissenter being a member of the corporation. A desire to obtain their freedom has existed amongst the inhabitants, but being generally of the Roman Catholic persuasion, they were deterred from applying for admission by a feeling that, on that ground alone, they would be rejected. When, about 1832, a Roman Catholic resident made the attempt and failed, this fortified the impression. In a district where the proportion of Roman Catholic to other sects was thirty to one, the sectarian feeling of the corporation has produced general odium towards the body.' The fact that the corporation members were non-resident was a further cause of annoyance as their task was to govern, and to hold the borough court.

But the inhabitants of Naas were unhappy with their masters for another important reason. Over the years they had seen the ownership of the corporation lands, including the important commons and the rents, being sequestered by the very officials who were supposed to oversee the interests of the townspeople. As the 4th Lord Mayo was then absent from Ireland it was not possible for the Inquiry to have access to all of the accounts, but it was observed that 'the expenses of erecting the new market house were charged against the corporation in the first account, although there is a stone in the building, on which is engraved a statement that it was built at the expense of Lord Mayo.'

The 4th Earl and his countess, who was a lady-in-waiting to Queen Adelaide, were not blessed with an heir and the title devolved on a nephew, Robert Bourke, who became the 5th Earl of Mayo in 1849. In 1847 his son, Robert Southwell Bourke, who was destined to be the 6th earl in 1867, was elected to represent Naas in parliament. It was later said that during his ten years in office 'that Naas corporation property was formerly much more extensive that it is at present; and that the portions of which have passed from the corporation have got into the possession of Lord Naas.'

In the House of Commons he rarely spoke on any subject but the Irish question. He was quoted as saying that 'he came from a family that cast in their lot with the Irish people, and during the famine he was never out of the saddle in his endeavours to arrange relief work and fund raising.' At the age of thirty, in 1852, Robert Southwell was appointed Chief Secretary for Ireland, an office which he held for three periods. While holding the title of Lord Naas he was Master of the Kildare foxhounds, and he was credited with much constructive work in the improvement of the hunt; but during his mastership there was a most distressing happening in the kennel. As the huntsman crossed the yard one summer day he saw a famous bitch hound with his baby of a few months in her mouth. She was taking the infant to her puppies. He rescued the child, which was unhurt, went into the house and got his gun and shot the bitch. The Master approved of the huntsman's actions when he was told the story.

A more amusing hunt incident was the confusing of an hotelier from Bray, County Wicklow, with Bray near Athy, where a meet of the hunt was to take place. The hotelier offered the hunt breakfast in his establishment on the day of the meet. Lord Naas wrote to thank him: 'Dear Proprietor of the Grand Hotel, Bray, Your Bray is not our Bray, neither is

*Lord Naas, Master of the Kildare Hunt 1857-1862*

our Bray your Bray. Yours truly, Naas.' Naas was also a keen horse breeder, and the stud he established at Palmerstown, the first commercial breeding operation in Ireland, had a high reputation. The annual sale of yearlings from the stud, which took place at the Curragh during the June race week, attracted a large number of purchasers, and contributed to the success of the Meeting.

In 1867 he had succeeded as 6th Earl of Mayo, and in the following year, as Chief Secretary, he was amongst the welcoming party for the Prince and Princess of Wales when they visited Punchestown. Indeed, when Queen Victoria, who was not pleased that the prince was again going to Ireland, said 'I much regret that the occasion should be the races, as it naturally strengthens the belief, already too prevalent, that your chief object is amusement,' the prince replied 'I am very anxious, dear Mama, that you should fully understand that I go there not for my amusement, but as a duty... Lord Mayo has particularly asked me to come.' That year Mayo was dubbed a Knight of St Patrick, and appointed as Viceroy of India.

During his four years in that office he was regarded as a wise and hard-working Viceroy, but it was said that he always longed for Ireland. When it came to erecting a memorial over the unnamed dead in India he had an Irish Cross made, and he requested that a similar monument should be put over his own grave when the time came.

It came sooner than he could have expected as, when he was visiting the Andaman Islands in 1872, he was assassinated by an escaped convict. His remains were received in state in Dublin, and a photograph, attributed to the Dublin photographer Chancellor, shows the departure of the horse-drawn draped catafalque on Eden Quay with a mounted military escort, and a great crowd of onlookers, some of whom have scaled the rigging of the vessel at the quay side. In his home place it was traditionally believed that he had been shipped home in a barrel of rum, which was said to have been drained and consumed by the sailors during the journey! As he had wished, he was buried beneath a Celtic Cross at Johnstown, and in a tribute to his memory the family home at Palmerstown was rebuilt by public subscription, and a plaque placed over the door to commemorate the event.

The heir to Palmerstown was Dermot Robert Wyndham Bourke, 7th Earl of Mayo. With Lord Drogheda, he was on the welcoming party, which also included Percy La Touche and Ambrose More O'Ferrall, at Punchestown when the Prince and Princess

*Dermot R W Bourke, 7th Earl of Mayo, President of the Kildare Archaeological Society in 1899*

of Wales again attended the Meeting in 1885. That day the racing was described as 'not good,' and the Hunt Cup was won by Henry de Robeck, despite a fall at the first fence.

It was the 7th Earl who convened the meeting which led to the establishment of the *County Kildare Archaeological Society* at Palmerstown in 1891. He was later president of the Society, and he wrote papers for the journal as well as a history of the Kildare Hunt.

Daisy Fingall, wife of Lord Fingall of Killeen Castle, County Meath, was a friend of Lady Mayo, and she recalled in her book *Seventy Years Young* their first journey in a motor car. It was in 1894 with Horace Plunkett: 'Horace had introduced into Ireland the very first motor-car to be seen in the country, and he drove about the quiet lanes at the terrifying speed of ten or twelve miles an hour, being frequently stopped for furious driving by an apologetic R.I.C. man. I have some old photographs of this first motor-car, and very uncomfortable it looks, one of Horace in it, and one of myself, Lady Mayo and Father Finlay as passengers. Our hats, including Father Finlay's clerical one, are tied on with enormous veils! We are all just about to start on one of our expeditions.'

In the Local Government elections of 1899 Lord Mayo was not elected and he went to London, having let Palmerstown to a tenant for a few months. From London he expressed his views on the subject of local government, and subsequently the *Daily Express* commented: 'He thinks it is a great misfortune that the country gentlemen who have for many years administered and been identified with county government should have been so completely ousted from their position...they had spent years on Grand Juries and Boards of Guardians, and worked well with the most violent nationalists.' But when Mayo predicted that 'the gentry who had been treated with such contemptuous rudeness would be unlikely to offer their services a second time' the journalist in the *Express* thought that 'in five or six years hence the people will look once more in many instances to the leisured classes to assist them in managing their local affairs.'

However a few years later Lady Mayo was also to suffer a rebuff when, as a member of the ladies' committee for visiting boarded-out children, she was prevented from visiting certain children by the woman with whom they were boarded. Lady Mayo told the Naas Guardians that 'Mrs Jones informed me that Fr Norris had lately been there, and had told her to tell me that this place was in his parish, and that I was not to visit the children any more.'

The 7th Earl and his Countess were enthusiastic supporters of the promotion of craft work; they founded the *Arts & Crafts Society of Ireland*, and the Countess also refounded the *Irish School of Art Needlework,* the aim of which was 'to provide suitable work for impoverished gentlewomen.' By 1901 there were twenty-three pupils in the school. She procured commissions from Queen Victoria, one for the private chapel at Windsor, and another for an altar frontal for St Patrick's Cathedral, Dublin. The altar frontal for St Brigid's Cathedral, Kildare, was also made by the School, and all three were designed by the English church architect John Ninian Comper. During the Great War, Daisy Fingall recalled, 'Geraldine Mayo's School of Art had been busy embroidering that flag (for the proposed Irish Brigade), but alas! it was returned to us. Questions were asked in the House about that incredibly stupid and hurtful gesture.'

Lady Mayo encouraged the opening of a carpet-making factory at Naas, and she was also supportive of Bridget Lawlor, a former employee at Palmerstown, when she opened a restaurant at Poplar Square, Naas, in 1913. She brought her friend Sir James Power of John's Lane Distillery to dine there, and so the standard of the establishment was accepted. It later developed into the celebrated Lawlor's Hotel.

Honoured with the appointment of senator in the new Free State, Mayo suffered for this distinction in 1923 when his house was burned down. The *Freeman's Journal* of 31 January

reported on the 'wanton havoc of a stately Irish edifice given to the flames.'The report continued that 'an orderly officer of the Irish Republican Army said that the party had come to
burn the house as a reprisal for the execution of six men at the Curragh.' Lord Mayo was
allowed to take some of his most cherished possessions from the house before it was sprinkled
with petrol and set ablaze. As well as the family records, relics from India, Africa, America and
Sardinia, and a fine collection of furniture, were destroyed. Lady Fingall commented on the
burning: 'Because Lord Mayo was a senator, they came to burn Palmerstown, wearing, several
of them, since it was a cold night, the woollen jerseys Lady Mayo had just given them. There
was time to save either her pearls in her bedroom, or her fowl in coops under the dining room
window, where they would, inevitably, be roasted alive. I think her pearls were not insured.
She hesitated only a second. Saved the fowl, and the pearls went.'After the fire Lady Mayo was
reported as having gone to stay with some friends in the neighbourhood, but Lord Mayo had
decided to occupy a gamekeeper's cottage on his estate. Asked if he would now go and live in
England he replied firmly: 'No, I will not be driven from my own country.'

Palmerstown was rebuilt with compensation from the state, but it was soon sold. Five
years later Lady Fingall wrote: 'Lady Mayo is a fine woman as I know. I wish we saw more
of her. How clearly she sees through the people to whom she has devoted her life, and
how splendid her acceptance of the facts and her courage in facing them.'

When Lady Mayo died in England in 1944 her obituary praised her work for the arts
and for home nursing units, quoting her as saying that 'her greatest pleasure was helping lame dogs over stiles.' Lord Mayo had died in London, aged seventy-seven, in 1927.
Terence Patrick Bourke, 10th and present Earl of the County Mayo lives in England. But
the Irish connection remains, with the birth in 1975 at Galway Regional Hospital of a
daughter to Máire (née Cronnolly) and Lord Charles Naas.

Palmerstown is now being developed as a hotel and golf course.

## Moore of Moore Abbey

An eighteenth century ballad titled *Whalley's Embarkation,* purporting to describe the
departure of the celebrated Buck Whalley for his walk to Jerusalem in 1788, included
references to some of his companions who had come to see him embark on the journey:
'*Lord Naas was there,*' and also '*Moore, that dirty whelp, I'm sure will lend a help!*' Lord Naas
was the Right. Hon. John Bourke from Palmerstown, Naas, and the gentleman referred to
in so uncomplimentary a manner was Lord Drogheda, an army officer who in 1762 had
been sent into disturbed districts in the province of Munster in command of a force by
whom many of the insurgents were stated to have been killed.

*Moore Abbey
in 1794
from Grose's
Antiquities of
Ireland*

The Moore family had come to Ireland as soldiers of fortune in Elizabethan times, and their association with this county can be traced back to the marriage in the early seventeenth century of Viscount Garret Moore of Mellifont, County Louth, to Mary Colley, the daughter of Sir Henry Colley of Castle Carbery. Another reference to the Moores at that period is found in Cardinal Moran's *Persecutions of Irish Catholics*, published in 1884. It tells that in 1641 'Francis More, son of Viscount Mellifont, at Blackhall, (Clane), committed a horrible massacre of old men, women and children, and transfixed the little infants on their mother's breasts with his swords and lances. Having spent the night with some of his officers in the house (Clongowes) of a noble lady whose husband was absent, he was treated with splendid hospitality and costly presents; but when the lady followed him to the door to bid him adieu on his departure, he ordered a rope to be thrown around her neck, and hanged her before her own door'. However, in the authoritative Sir Bernard Burke's *Peerage & Baronetage,* published in 1887, the Christian name Francis is not found in the family in that century. Nevertheless, writing in the *Journal of the County Kildare Archaeological Society,* Fr Matthew Devitt S.J. identifies the unfortunate lady as ninety-year old Mrs Mary Eustace, née Wogan, who was living at Clongowes.

Another curious anecdote about the family was that the horse ridden by King Billy at the Battle of the Boyne subsequently came into the ownership of Henry, 3rd Earl of Drogheda. He had the animal stuffed and draped in cloth of gold, and years later, when the fourth Earl was forced to sell the family home at Mellifont, and came to Moore Abbey, he brought with him the horse, draped in the cloth of gold. To quote Barry Walsh of the Monasterevan Historical Society (History Ireland Winter 2004), 'no doubt it became an unusual attraction for members of the Orange Order, an organisation with whom the Droghedas became associated, Monasterevan having one of the leading Lodges in Kildare in the 1790s. In the nineteenth century when a land steward of the Droghedas was emigrating to Australia, he took a piece of the caparison with him. There he found that it was identified as a valuable piece of real cloth of gold.'

The 5th Earl of Drogheda, with his son the Hon. and Revd Edward Moore, was lost on the passage from Wales to Dublin in 1758. His successor, Charles the 6th Earl, built the Gothic mansion of Moore Abbey, Monasterevan in the mid-eighteenth century, on the site of a medieval Cistercian abbey which had come into the Moore family through

*Marquis of Drogheda, member of the Turf Club and prominent in the establishment of Punchestown*

marriage in 1699. Charles was created Marquis of Drogheda in 1791, and he also held the office of joint Post-Master-General.

The Hon. Ponsonby Moore, another son of the ill-fated 5th earl of Drogheda, named his estate at Newbridge, *Moorefield,* and part of that estate was leased to the War Department for the building of the cavalry barracks at Newbridge in 1812.

Some decades later Thomas Lacy from Wexford, who was touring the county by train in the autumn of 1855, visited Newbridge where he admired 'the thriving new military dominated town, the evidence of taste and comparative refinement, the detached groups of cottages, for the most part thatched, and with gardens, the ivy-covered Protestant church, and the demesne of *Moorefield,* the residence of Ponsonby Moore Esq.'

Sir Henry Francis Seymour Moore, the 3rd Marquis of Drogheda, who was listed in the *The Monthly Military Directory of the Curragh Camp and Newbridge* for December 1887, was then one of the most important figures in the sporting world of the turf, both flat and steeplechase. A Steward of the Turf Club for thirty-six years, and a respected breeder and trainer, he had also held the office of Curragh Ranger during which time he sought to protect the sward by keeping the soldiers and the graziers in check.

Moore Abbey, during the lifetime of the 3rd Marquis and his Marchioness, was celebrated for its hospitality, such as the grand ball held there in January 1876: 'There was a huge attendance at the ball, including the Officer Commanding the Curragh District, Maj. Gen. and Mrs Seymour, his *aide-decamp,* and officers from the Queen's Bays and Royal Artillery from Newbridge. From the Curragh came officers of the 17th Regiment and Depot, of the 45th and 62nd regiments, Col. Dunne and officers of the 99th Regiment and Depot. Mr D. O'Connor and officers of the Control Department, officers of the Royal Engineers etc.' But there was a realisation on the part of guests who were invited to stay at Moore Abbey that it was a very cold house. When John Henry Reginald Scott, 4th Earl of Clonmell from Bishopscourt, Straffan, came to stay at Moore Abbey, he brought 'an exceptionally heavy portmanteau with him in his luggage which, as the footmen were struggling to get it up the stairs, burst open and was found to be full of coal.'

When the 3rd Marquis died, on the eve of Irish Derby Day in 1892, he was mourned as 'a great loss to the sport which he had worked so hard to promote and reform.' It was decided that, as a testimony to his work, the *Drogheda Memorial Fund* would be established to erect a hospital 'for the permanent and temporary relief of trainers and riders when in necessitous circumstances, arising from age, sickness, accident, or misfortune, and also the widows and children of such persons.' *The Drogheda Memorial Hospital* was opened on the edge of the Curragh in 1899, and it still continues in a caring function.

Henry Charles Ponsonby Moore succeeded his father as 10th Earl of Drogheda in 1908 and he had two children, Charles Garret Ponsonby and Patricia Doreen. In England he held many positions, as a lieutenant in the Irish Guards, as a clerk in the Foreign Office from 1907 to 1917, and as a representative peer for Ireland. Divorced in 1921, the Earl did not live at Moore Abbey, Monasterevan, which he found had become difficult to maintain. After an ownership of some 300 years he sold Moore Abbey to the *Sisters of Charity of Jesus & Mary,* prior to which it was for a time home to the tenor Count John McCormack. Henry, who was succeeded by his son Charles Garret in 1957, later wrote that the sale of Moore Abbey was completed in early 1940 but the nuns did not move in until after the War. He claimed it was sold for little more than £5,000 but that this in effect meant a saving of £500 a year for maintenance! His son, Charles Garrett Ponsonby Moore, 11th Earl of Drogheda (1910–1990), was from 1945 to 1975, successively Managing Director and Chairman of *The Financial Times.* His sister Patricia, who had married an actor named

Ahern, the brother of an Irish army officer, died following a fall from a window at the Shelbourne Hotel in Dublin. The present and 12th Earl of Drogheda, Derry Moore, is a society photographer in London.

Another Moore family, which had its origins in Clonmel, County Tipperary, but was later through marriage to be connected to the Drogheda family, built Killashee, the Victorian Jacobean house on 200 acres near Naas, in 1860. Though imposing externally, the house is over embellished both internally and externally with the family crest, but the plaster, wood and stonework of the interior is of the highest quality, a reminder of the skills of the craftsmen of that time. The motto displayed there is: *Unless the Lord buildeth this house, the labour is in vain.*

This report in the *Irish Times* of that Opening Meet reads like a *Who's Who* of the county notables. The occupants of the carriages of Lords Clonmell and Cloncurry were listed, and also there were 'Mr Fortescue Tynte, Hon. E. Lawless, Capt. R. Mansfield, Mr T. Conolly MP, Mr Percy La Touche and the Marquis of Drogheda.....a platoon of military men, led by General Seymour from the Curragh, were there, with Mr Knox and the Horse Artillery from Newbridge. There were parties from the country houses of Killashee, Straffan, and the Hon. Charles Bourke's bijou hunting box Roseboro'. The Squire of Castletown and Mr Edmund Mansfield represented their dynasties, while Captain St Leger Moore was described as forsaking his wonted pastimes of tent-pegging, lemon slicing, and all those Indian feats of horsemanship for which his regiment is celebrated, to return for the season in Kildare. Nearly 300 half-crowns were subscribed in cap-money.'

Of course the County gentry welcomed the officers, many of whom they knew from their own service in the army or militia, or through family connections. The hunting field greatly benefited from the military, and the racecourse and point-to-points, the polo grounds, cricket pitches, and shooting parties likewise prospered. The gentry also enjoyed the seasonal balls and other entertainments in the Curragh camp, to which they were always invited.

Capt. Richard St Leger Moore, 5th Lancers, was *aide-de-camp* to Maj. Gen. Seymour, Commanding the Curragh District in 1880, and Master of the Kildare Hunt from 1883 to 1897. His wife was Alice Tynte of Tynte Park, Dunlavin, whose older sister was married to Capt. Henry Moore of Moorefield, Newbridge, and a great-grand-son of the 5th Earl of Drogheda.

When St Leger Moore relinquished the position of Master of the Hunt, after a successful thirteen seasons, he was presented with this verse:

> The ladies who love and follow the chase,
> From Dublin to Enfield, from Newbridge to Naas,
> Have joined in this tribute to sport in Kildare,
> Wishing joy to our Master and luck to his heir.

His home at Killashee was well known for the big dinner parties he hosted, opportunities, no doubt, for the fair young ladies to meet exciting young military men. In 1901, as was the case in most of the big houses, the labour in the household was dominantly Protestant, with only one Catholic amongst the staff of eleven.

But the golden days were coming to an end. In March 1919 *Sinn Fein* proposed that hunting should be disrupted, and at a Meet of the Kildare hounds a crowd of people surrounded the hunt. Lt Col. St Leger Moore afterwards said, 'that the hounds were beaten, the horses struck, and the riders, including a reverend gentleman, were assaulted and pelted with stones.' He added, 'that the windows of the home of the master of the hounds had been broken, and he warned that if politics invaded sport that not only hunting, but also racing, cricket and football would be affected.' Hunting was then temporarily suspended.

In October 1921 St Leger Moore died by his own hand; the *Leinster Leader* reporting 'the tragic suddenness of his death,' said 'it was the passing of a valuable link between the old county family traditions and the more democratic thought of to-day.' The former hospitable house of Killashee became a convent and a school in 1927, and when the 500 acre estate was broken-up by the Land Commission four years later the convent was left with 85 acres. The sisters recalled, 'When Major Richard Moore sold Killashee he did not forget his old estate workers. All the labourers got a pension of £1 a month, and a quarter ton of coal a month. All of the houses were given to the tenants after one and a half years.' Now the *La Sainte Union Des Sacresoeurs* are gone, and Killashee has resumed its hospitable role, but as a hotel.

## Stratford of Belan

The Stratford family had come to Ireland from England in the mid seventeenth century and purchased land in Kildare and Wicklow, eventually creating an estate of 28,000 acres in Wicklow and Kildare, they were connected through marriage with the Eustaces of Castlemartin and Harristown.

In the latter half of the eighteenth century John Stratford, Baron of Baltinglass, Member of Parliament, and Sheriff of the counties Wicklow, Kildare, Carlow and Wexford, was created Earl of Aldborough. Belan, Aldborough's seat, situated a few miles from Ballytore on the Dublin to Castledermot road, was designed by the celebrated architects Richard Castle and Francis Bindon. William Ashford's paintings of Belan in 1781 give a very romantic impression of the great house and its gardens.

The mansion, and the cotton industry village which he established at Stratford-upon-Slaney, were depicted in Taylor & Skinners *Maps of the Roads of Ireland* when it was published in 1777, and to which the Earl subscribed for two copies. Stratford-upon-Slaney, four miles north of Baltinglass, was planned to be a manufacturing town which would have streets and a square, with public lighting. There was to be a library, and three churches: Protestant, Roman Catholic and Presbyterian. A weekly market and regular fairs were to be held. By 1786 the building of the new town was completed, and the Earl put it up for sale. It was purchased by an entrepreneur named Orr who established a cotton and calico industry, but despite the change of ownership the enterprise failed, and it was closed by 1860.

In 1798 Aldborough raised 'two Corps on permanent duty at Belan, Timolin, Castle Dermot and Baltinglass'. In his journal he described 1798 as 'the most unhappy year of

*Belan House in 1781 from an oil painting by Ashford*

my life. Dismissed soldiers as United Irishmen, though yeomen, on their own confession. Several of my corps dismissed as disaffected. Two of them shot for it.' The turmoil also affected Lady Aldborough. After the battle of Stratford-on Slaney she saved the life of the parish priest of Baltinglass by throwing herself between him and a group of angry yeomen intent on killing him.

But Aldborough was an eccentric character and, following a row with a neighbour about their boundaries, he spent six months in jail. His successor at Belan was also eccentric, and was remembered for greeting his guests: 'When do you intend to depart?' As a member of parliament he was described as 'a slippery customer.' The 4th Earl, who was noted for having had a duel with a fellow officer, was referred to in his brother's will as 'the vapouring Captain Stratford'. But he was also known as 'the inventor earl' as he set about the making of a balloon at Stratford Lodge, Baltinglass. When the house was burned down, and his plans for making the balloon destroyed, the earl went to live in the balloon house. But, according to Lord Walter FitzGerald 'owing to his reckless gambling and extravagant mode of living, the property became heavily mortgaged, and from the year 1823 commenced the ruin and decay of the place.'

Belan was described in 1837 as 'an extensive pile of buildings, situated at the foot of Bolton Hill and occupying the site of an ancient castle which formerly belonged to a branch of the FitzGerald family, and was destroyed by Cromwell. In the house is preserved an ancient bed, in which James II and William III successively slept in the year 1690.'

A lady who had visited Belan in early Victorian times recalled that 'the grand entrance was approached from Moone by a long avenue, with a wide piece of grass on either side, with trees at the back, very handsome and about a mile in length. The grounds were very beautiful, and of considerable extent. On one side, though not seen were the celebrated fish-ponds (not that in my time there were any fish in them), large and deep, the trees around giving them a secluded and fascinating look. Here on hot summer's evenings we used to sit and watch the dragon flies. The house was always filled with guests. A French chef by name Durant, whose recipes I use to this day, and much prefer to any others, reigned supreme in the kitchens, where immense numbers of people of all sorts and conditions fed. In fact open house was kept, and a reign of reckless extravagance began. Racing, cock-fighting, card playing, gambling, in fact all the amusements then in vogue, were the order of the day. The stables were filled with magnificent horses, and I have heard, at the time of the Curragh races the splendour of the Belan equipages, the horses, the new and gorgeous liveries of the postillions and out-riders, together with the dresses of the ladies, was a sight yearly looked forward to by the whole county.'

That lady lived to see the house in ruins: 'the wind blowing where it listeth, sighs over the desolate grounds and gardens, once so beautiful. A herd lives in the yard, sole occupant of that once lovely demesne. Thus has passed away a race once great, wealthy, and powerful; their names and their place are known no more. *Sic transit gloria mundi'*.

The 5th Earl was described by an historian of the family as 'a scoundrel who brought about the ruin of Belan, and a bigamist.' Not surprisingly, another chronicler titled his paper on the family *The Eccentric Earls of Aldborough*. The earldom became extinct in 1875, and now the only remaining features of the great estate are a couple of obelisks and a rotunda temple in the fields.

Aldborough House at Portland Row in Dublin, one of the city's most significant eighteenth century Georgian townhouses, is still there, though its interior has been much damaged by use at different periods over the centuries as a school, a barracks and a post office depot. In 2001 the mansion was acquired by the Irish Music Rights Organisation and its restoration initiated.

# 6

# de Burghs and de Robecks

The Rt. Revd Ulysses Burgh of Dromkeen, County Limerick, whose father had conformed to the Protestant Church, deserted the cause of King James II for that of William of Orange. As a result his house was burned, but he was rewarded with the Bishopric of Ardagh in 1692. Two of his sons, who served in the king's army, later acquired estates in County Kildare where their descendants continued to provide men for the Church and the Colours.

His eldest son, Revd Rickard Burgh, Dromkeen, had a son named Thomas who married his cousin Mary Burgh of Oldtown, Naas, a daughter of Thomas Burgh. In time their daughter Mary married Capt. Philpot Wolfe of Forenaghts, Naas, in 1753, thus uniting two Kildare gentry families. William, the second son of the Revd Ulysses Burgh, built the classical mansion of Bert, near Athy, between 1725 and 1730. He held the office of Comptroller & Accountant General. His grandson, also named William, married Mary Warburton, the heiress of Firmount, Clane, while Thomas, another grandson, was an MP, and he also in time held the same offices as had his grandfather.

Thomas's eldest son was Gen. Sir Ulysses Burgh, 2nd Baron Downes, who served as *aide-de-camp* to Wellington in the Peninsular War, and in the same capacity to both King George IV and King William IV. He was later Surveyor-general of ordnance, and an Irish Representative Peer from 1833-63.

*Bookplate of Thomas Burgh, Oldtown, Naas 1722*

Just after Christmas 1839 Lord Downes was in the chair at a meeting convened in Athy Court House to consider the best way of relieving the distressed state of the poor in the locality. It was decided to issue an appeal to enable fuel, straw and clothing to be purchased for the needy, and his lordship opened the subscription with a donation of £10, and soon a total of £100 was reached.

Lord Downes assumed the surname de Burgh in 1848, and fittingly, his two daughters married peers! The eldest daughter married the 3rd Earl of Clonmell of Bishopscourt, Kill, and when his second daughter married Lord Seaton they lived at Bert, Athy.

The third son of the Bishop of Ardagh was Colonel Thomas Burgh, the Surveyor-General for Ireland who, when he purchased almost 3,000 acres near Naas at the end of the seventeenth century established a family connection with the County town which has continued to the present time. The Burgh family facilitated the building of the first post-Reformation Catholic Church in Naas in the mid eighteenth century, and the site of the present church of Our Lady & St David, and of the former Mercy Convent, are chronicled as the *Burgh Donation*.

Col. Thomas Burgh's *Map Book of 1722* shows that he was by then a major landlord of the town. Remembered as the architect of the Dublin barracks (now the National Museum at Collins barracks), Steven's Hospital and the library of Trinity College, he was also involved in the construction of the forts in Cork harbour and of the tower of the Royal Hospital complex at Kilmainham. High Sheriff of County Kildare and Member of Parliament for Naas, in 1712 he leased a pew in St David's church, Naas, and established a permanent link between Oldtown and St David's. Many of his descendants were clergy-men, and two were vicars of Naas, one of whom restored the ruinous St David's castle as a Rectory. Another was a Roman Catholic priest in England.

At Oldtown Burgh planned and commenced to build the country's first Palladian winged house, but it was never completed. The part originally occupied was destroyed by fire in 1955, and the family now lives in the reconstructed remaining pavilion. Thomas Burgh died in 1730, but surprisingly, his burial place is not known. A pyramidal vault at the Maudlins cemetery, Naas, is a de Burgh burial place. Over the cemetery gate a plaque dated 1782 is inscribed to Lord Mayo who 'bequeathed a lasting habitation not made with hands.'

Above left: *The Burgh Arms*

Above right: *Oldtown, the de Burgh ancestral home which was accidentally destroyed by fire in the 1950s*

Elizabeth Burgh, the eldest daughter of the Surveyor-general, married Ignatius Hussey of Donore, Caragh, Naas, who had conformed to the Protestant church in 1718. Their son Walter assumed the name Burgh when he inherited the Dromkeen, County Limerick, property in 1762. From his election as M.P. for Athy, on the nomination of the Duke of Leinster in 1768, he was patriotic, and took an active interest in government, and he was supportive of his fellow Roman Catholic countrymen. The Popery Laws he described as 'a cruel code, not founded, as some assert, in necessary policy, but religious persecution. Ireland is a subordinate country, and its great object is to guard against the oppressions of England. The power of avoiding that oppression is in proportion to the ultimate power of resisting it by force. Whenever such opposition is to be made, it must begin with the Protestants; but they, being too few, cannot hazard it without the Papists, who would enter into no cordial bond of union with Protestant manacles on their hands. While we remain thus jealous of each other, we are but a colony of Americans with the Indians at our backs.' Holding the legal rank of Prime Serjeant from 1776, Hussey Burgh was noted for his eloquence. Of him, Henry Flood said: 'He did not live to be ennobled, he was ennobled by nature.'

An outsider's opinion of another member of the Burgh family was that of William St Leger Alcock, an officer stationed at Naas military barracks in 1832. He went to a service in St David's Church 'for the first time and was not at all edified by the sermon of a Mr Burg,' who was Walter Burgh, the Vicar of Naas.

Whatever about the quality of the vicar's sermons, it is unlikely that any criticisms could be made of Lady Catherine Burgh's management of affairs at Oldtown. In recent times her housekeeping notebook for 1834 to 1838 came up for sale; described as 'ruled in red, some notes-tipped in, numerous pages scored in ink, and listing the contents of the family seat, and tenants' wages accounts,' it was priced at €950.

The vicar's elder brother Thomas was Dean of Cloyne, whose wife was a sister of the 3rd Earl of Donoughmore. Henry and Robert, two of their sons, emigrated to Australia in 1841 and, having survived shipwreck, they settled in the colony where to-day their homestead is regarded as one of the oldest continuously occupied colonial dwellings in Western Australia. Henry returned home in 1847 to marry Elizabeth Louisa Hendrick of Kerdiffstown, Naas, and consequently became related to two other Kildare families, the Borrowes and the Aylmers.

Some years before the brothers emigrated their cousin Edward Hussey Burgh had settled in the colony, and he was farming 10,680 acres at Spring Hill. There they were also happy to meet a couple named Wilkinson from Naas, as Mrs Wilkinson had for many years been a servant of their uncle Walter Burgh. In 1981 a descendant of Robert Burgh wrote an account of those pioneering days in the new colony.

During the famine years of the 1840s the de Burgh family organised relief measures in their area. Walter Burgh, Vicar of Naas, was Treasurer of the Relief Committee. His nephew Henry, returned from Australia, initiated a scheme to provide employment in the county. Within a couple of years twenty-three men were employed on the 1,350-acre Oldtown estate.

The Oldtown estate is well documented. In 1924 Lt. Col. T. J. de Burgh commenced a *History of Oldtown* (in his old *Army Book 134*) in which the details of the enlargement of the house and the making of the gardens, as well as much other material, is recorded. He noted 'In March 1899 Oldtown was one of the oldest Heronries in Ireland, there were ten nests. In the great storm of 1903 the nests were blown down and the Herons have never returned to nest.' He continued: 'The rookery from Turrets to Main lodge enabled us to shoot with a pea-rifle up to 100 rooks in a day. In 1910 the year Mrs Tandy died at Oldtown the rooks forsook the whole demesne although they nested on ash trees on the Monread side of Sallins road. No rooks nested at Oldtown 'till about 1917 when they began to return. We used to have owls but since 1871 none have been seen. On the night of 14 July 1871 (two members of the family) heard and saw a large white owl flying backwards and forwards under Mrs de Burgh's window, screaming like a baby. Mrs de Burgh died on 19 July 1871.'

Mrs Tandy was a sister of T. J. de Burgh who had married a neighbour, Commander Dashwood Goldie Tandy, R.N., The Knocks, Naas. He had died suddenly in October 1883 while driving with his wife to visit the Baron de Robeck at Gowran Grange. They had got out of the trap to walk up a hill, and when they got back into the trap he remarked that since he was in the East Indies the exertion of walking up a hill always told upon him. Then he collapsed and expired in his wife's arms.

At the age of sixty-two in 1914 Col. T.J. de Burgh, who had served in the Boer War fifteen years before, drove his Rover to France to join the Indian Corps as a dispatch rider, and while there he managed to meet frequently his son Eric. Another son, Tommy, had joined the 5th Lancers at Marlborough Barracks in Dublin in August 1914 when his sister Coralie came up from Naas with the kit and equipment which she had collected for him: 'Sir Kildare Borrowes (of Barretstown Castle) contributed a cavalry sword, Col. Richard St Leger Moore (of Killashee) a very smart pair of khaki breeches, leather saddles, camp equipment etc.' On the day that his father arrived in France twenty-six year old Tommy went missing on a reconnaissance mission, and was never found.

Brigade Major Eric de Burgh 9th Bengal Lancers, Hodson's Horse, from 'somewhere in Loos' on 3 February 1916 wrote to his father at home in Oldtown. 'I am just completing my tenth day in this dugout and we go out on 7th. We came in for bombardments on 26th, 27th and 28th, and the one of 27th was particularly lively; but the trenches are far better that any we have been in before and the casualties much less than could have been expected. Our machine guns got into the brutes several times while out working and on one occasion after they had been located by a patrol an officer and a NCO dragged a machine gun out along the top of a sap and opened on them at short range, 14 corpses were found there next morning. The same NCO bagged eight another time and has been recommended for a DCM.'

*General Sir Eric de Burgh*

Having soldiered in the South African War and the First World War, General Sir Eric de Burgh was Chief of the General Staff in India from 1939 to 1941. He later recalled his earlier days in India when he was officer-in-charge of elephants during the visit of the Viceroy, Lord Hardinge, to Delhi in 1912. An anarchist made an attempt on the Viceroy and 'the whole of the right side of the back of the howdah was blown out, and the terribly mutilated body of the unfortunate Balrampur Jemadar (who had been my right hand-man throughout) who had been holding up the state umbrella over the Viceroy, was hanging down over the elephant's back.' He saw that 'Lord Hardinge was almost fainting, and Lady Hardinge very white but quite calm; she is a plucky woman.' She was got down and given some brandy, while Lord Hardinge was attended to in the howdah.

When Gen. de Burgh retired he settled back at home in Naas, and he took an active part in the *County Kildare Archaeological Society*, being President for many years. The family had long association with the society, Archdeacon de Burgh having been an inaugural member in 1891 and Thomas de Burgh had compiled a history of Naas for the Society's journal.

The transformation of the image and interests of this long established County family is now evident in that the internationally known singer Chris de Burgh is a son of Gen. de Burgh's daughter Maeve Davison, and that Chris's daughter Rosanna captured the *Miss Ireland* and *Miss World* titles in 2003. Major John de Burgh, the present owner of Oldtown, joined the Ayrshire Yeomanry in 1939, and later, after transferring to 16/5th Lancers, served in North Africa where he was awarded a Military Cross. After the war he developed the Oldtown estate and there he trained his own horses and opened a stud farm, as well as serving on the Punchestown Management Committee, the Racing Board, and as a steward of the Turf Club.

Hunting three days a week, Maj. de Burgh, with a few other remaining members of the gentry, saw the hunts transformed from 'their old neighbourly status into commercial ventures with hired horses and too many riders.' The Oldtown estate has recently been sold, but the house and gardens remain with the family for the lifetime of the present owner, and the garden has been donated to the Naas Town Council.

Two other men of the family, Hubert and Charles had distinguished service in the Royal Navy in the Great War, both receiving DSOs. They both again served in the Second World War. Their two sisters, Coralie and Zoë, nursed in the Richmond Hospital in Dublin during the Great War, in which Coralie's fiancée died. Zoë married Ulsterman Capt. Thomas Kennedy Maxwell RN, and after the war was over they went to farm in Northern Rhodesia. Maxwell and his two sons fought in the Second World War, following which he bought a house on the Curragh. One son, Lt Col. R. M. Maxwell, has recently compiled and edited some of his mother's documents and titled them *Zoë: The letters, Diaries and memorabilia of a Wicked Imperialist*. He describes his mother as 'a daughter of a family living not far from the Curragh Camp in Ireland, at that time the largest concentration of British troops in the British Isles. Not only does she follow the fortunes of members of her family through three wars, but also those of many friends who marched to war from the Curragh Camp.'

Capt. Charles de Burgh RN, brother to Zoë, served during the Great War in HM Submarine K22, and some of his experiences have been recorded by his daughter Coralie Kinahan in her historical novel *After the War came Peace*. She also introduces into her narrative another family member, Admiral Jack de Robeck of Gowran Grange, Naas, whose sister Emily was the wife of Lt Col. T.J. de Burgh, mother of the soldiers and sailors mentioned here, and grandmother to Lady Kinahan. In his book Maxwell writes '(grand) uncle Jack de Robeck was Admiral of Patrols 1912-1914, commanded the naval force at the

Dardanelles in 1915, and was subsequently Commander in Chief of the Mediterranean Fleet, and of the Atlantic Fleet 1922-1924 and Admiral of the Fleet 1925.'The admiral's two de Robeck nephews also soldiered in the Great War.

Col. Maxwell in his introduction says 'our global interests led to the establishment of families which specialised in the administration and defence of our homeland, and our interests abroad. Often imperial duties took their sons and daughters into danger and life in unhealthy places. These were no ordinary people. They were the warrior class of our nation. This breed of men and women are referred to by our politically motivated denigrators as *Wicked Imperialists*. Foreigners are fascinated to discover how many families of these *wicked imperialists* can trace an ancestry back through many centuries. Zoë's family, the de Burghs, is one such family which derived its name as a gift from the Emperor Charlemagne, at the siege of Burgos in Spain (in the eighth century).'

Lady Coralie Kinahan, whose father was Submarine Captain Charles de Burgh RN of Oldtown, recalled holidays there seventy years ago: 'We were kept up in the nursery most of the time except meals. We used to be taken for a walk immediately after breakfast and then put to rest under the big beech trees on the lawn in a collection of gorgeous Victorian and Georgian prams. Down in the stable yard the head groom, whose daughter was our very pretty nanny who all the sailors were keen on, used to show us the horses. Mummy stayed at Oldtown quite a lot during the First War when daddy was away at Scappa Flow, and she was there during the Irish Civil War when the Sinn Feiners came to burn down the house and were frightened away by grandfather's cold blue eyes and terrifying voice. They made the mistake of sending someone local to do the dirty job and grandfather was a magistrate and recognised them. Mummy said she always slept with a revolver under her pillow then, with which she was a crack shot, having been taught by her brothers.'

The paternal grandmother of Lydia and Coralie was Emily Anne de Robeck, daughter of the 4th Baron de Robeck of Gowran Grange, Naas. Of the Fock family, which was ennobled in Sweden in the mid eighteenth century, the 2nd Baron had married Anne FitzPatrick, an Irish heiress with estates in counties Kildare, Wicklow and Dublin.

The 2nd Baron, a former captain in *Schomberg's Drags* in the French Army, is remembered in Fergus D'Arcy's *Horses, Lords & Racing Men* as having in September 1799, 'in an hilarious pony race over four miles wagered his rival that he would ride without once sitting down in his saddle, or appear more blown than is usual with jockeys by profession. The Baron won his challenge, standing up in his stirrups in the true German Hussar fashion, and the day being fine, crowds came from all parts to see this extraordinary race.'

John, their only child, went on the customary Grand Tour to Italy, and his diary of that journey is amongst the extensive collection of family papers preserved at Gowran Grange. A decade later John had an unexpected adventure when he was captured by a French privateer while returning from service with Gen. Sir John Moore in Spain. But he survived, to become the 3rd Baron in 1817.

In his diary for 23 July 1820 the Baron described his first meeting with Mary Lawless, daughter of the 2nd Baron Cloncurry of Lyons, near Celbridge: 'Went to church at Kill. Met the Kennedy's and drove to Lyons. Saw nothing particularly pretty there except Miss Lawless, Lord Cloncurry's daughter. The view in the dining room of the Bay of Naples is very bad. Ordered the mare over from Whitlease. Col. & Mrs Maingay are to dinner'. A couple of weeks later he noted that 'Mary Lawless came to take leave of Eliza FitzClarence and spent greatest part of day with us. She is a pretty pleasing girl. Lord Errol proposed to Miss FitzClarence and is probably not refused'. On the 2 September the diarist recorded 'beautiful weather, sun quite warm. Rode with lovely Miss Lawless and her brother to

*4th Baron de Robeck, MFH of the Kildare Hunt*
*1862-1868*

Castletown and magnificent mansion belonging to Lady Louisa Conolly. Lord and Lady Cloncurry drove in their Tilbury.'

Four days later the Baron 'declared my sentiments with regard to Miss Lawless both to herself and father. Rode with them to Straffan, Mr Henry's place, and to Lodge Park. Returned home by Celbridge and weather beautiful. On the following day he watched the eclipse, which took place at half-past twelve. Passed greatest part of the day with my dear Mary who I really believe has a penchant for me. Within a couple of days: The die is cast; Mary signed a contract of marriage. I begged her to consider well what she was about. It is now her fault if she should repent of having given her consent. It shall be my study to make her happy and comfortable as I can. Three weeks later de Robeck rode with Lord Cloncurry to Dublin and signed my marriage settlements. Col. Plunket, Mrs Whalley and Mr and Mrs Garnet came to dinner.' On the following day he was married at 12 o'clock by Dean Langrish to 'my dear Mary'. Col. Plunket, Mrs Whalley and Mr and Mrs Garnet were present as also Lord and Lady Cloncurry. Mrs Whalley, the widow of the celebrated Buck Whalley, was a daughter of the first Baron Cloncurry, and an aunt of the bride.

Alas, within a decade the Baron and his *dear Mary* were divorced. Then in 1830 he married another lady from the neighbourhood, Emily Elizabeth Henry, the eldest daughter of John Joseph Henry of Straffan and his wife Lady Emily FitzGerald, daughter of the 2nd Duke of Leinster, and a niece of the patriot Lord Edward FitzGerald. The 3rd Baron de Robeck, who held the office of County High Sheriff, lived at Leixlip Castle, and there, in 1856 at the age of sixty-six, he was drowned in the Salmon Leap. His body was found at Lucan eleven days later.

So extravagant was John Joseph, he was forced to sell Straffan and go to live abroad. The house he had built at Straffan, and which included an underground passage from the house to the stables, was later demolished, and Hugh Barton afterwards built, on a different site, the house, which is now the core building of the *Kildare Hotel & Country Club*. John Joseph's younger brother Hugh married his cousin Anne Leeson, daughter of the 1st Earl of Milltown, and it was he who about 1770 built the classical Lodge Park, a smaller version of his wife's home, Russborough, County Wicklow. It was said that Hugh Henry intended his house to have a frontage as long as that of his father-in-law's Russborough!

John Henry Fock, the son of the ill-fated 3rd Baron, before inheriting the baronetcy, served in the army in India and South Africa, and some four hundred letters, which he wrote

*John Joseph Henry of Straffan, in the mid eighteenth century, portrait by Pompeo Batoni*

to his mother, are in the family archives. There also are his journals, telling of his travels to Paris and Switzerland in 1875. It was the 4th Baron who, from 1857 to 1859, built the gabled Tudor-Revival house at Gowran Grange on the estate, which in 1876 consisted of 1,838 acres. He was Chairman of the *Naas Young Men's Christian Association* in 1867 when it celebrated its fourth anniversary with a tea and concert in the Town Hall. A banner exclaiming '*Welcome, Baron, All welcome*' decorated the podium. The strong social relationship between the military and the gentry was apparent in 1887 when the 11th Hussars from Newbridge held their steeplechase at Gowran Grange, over a course selected by the baron.

General Sir Alexander Godley, who soldiered with the 1st Battalion Dublin Fusiliers on the Curragh about that time, socialised with the de Robecks. He later described the Baron as the 'father of the celebrated admiral, and of the late baron, who was a distinguished horse-gunner and subsequently master of foxhounds. His grandson, also a horse-gunner, carries on the sporting tradition of the family.' During the Boer War, as was customary for the ladies, his daughter Gertrude de Robeck assisted Lady Mayo in raising subscriptions for the *Soldiers' & Sailors' Families Association*.

The affection of the ladies for the royal family was apparent in the *Kildare Observer* report of the death and funeral of Queen Victoria in 1901. St David's Church in Naas 'was draped in purple and black, under the direction of Miss de Robeck, and the service was attended by the NCOs and men of the Naas Depot, and the constabulary, as well as the officers, who attended in full dress. The military of the Roman Catholic persuasion attended mass in the Catholic Church.' Nevertheless, the ethos of the de Robeck family was such that in 1901 no Roman Catholics were employed at Gowran Grange.

The 4th Baron was a captain in the 8th Foot and a major in the Kildare Militia; he was also Ranger of the Curragh, Deputy Lieutenant and Justice of the Peace for the County, and Master of the Kildare Hunt. His six seasons as MFH were described in the *Irish Times*: 'Just what a master of foxhounds should be, kind and jovial with the field, liberal with his purse, courteous and considerate to strangers, affable with the farmers, and bent upon showing sport if sport can be shown; and though last, not least, the best of landlords, which increases his popularity very much amongst the occupiers of land, who always welcome him wherever he goes.' The hunt also honoured him in Naas Town Hall with the presentation of two silver candelabras, while the people of Naas, non-members, presented him with a silver kettle.

The sporting spirit of the family was captured in a hunt ballad:

> There's a grand one to ride who as everyone knows
> Is troubled with neither the shakes nor the slows.
> With judgement that's true and a firm huntin' sate
> The baron de Robeck's a hard man to bate.

Sir John Michael de Robeck, second son of the 4th Baron, was a much-decorated Admiral of the Fleet who had commanded a naval force in the Dardanelles during the First World War, and afterwards was High Commissioner in Constantinople. His brother, Col. Henry Edward William Fock, 5th Baron, served in the Great War, and his daughters Olave and Harriet were also at the Front, with the Red Cross Motor Ambulance. The Baron had by then separated from his wife, and it was from his temporary home at Osberstown that his eldest daughter Dorothy Zoë married Major Digby Robert Peel, 60th Royal Artillery, in 1910. The 6th baron, a gunner, saw service in both world wars. He is remembered in the family as having always checked his watch against the regular boom of the signalling cannon from the Curragh Camp!

Gowran Grange is now the only estate of consequence (several hundreds of acres) in its original ownership remaining in county Kildare. The present owner is Charles John, the thirty-two year old 8th Baron de Robeck.

*The wedding of Dorothy Zoë de Robeck, daughter of the 5th Baron de Robeck, to Major Digby Robert Peel 60th Royal Artillery, of Alexandria, Egypt, at the de Robeck's temporary home, Osberstown, Naas, on 8 October 1910. The groomsman was Major Edward Conolly, 60th Royal Artillery of Castletown, Celbridge*

7

# Soldiers and Sportsmen

## Clements of Killadoon

Nathaniel Clements, banker, Member of Parliament and amateur architect, had in the mid-eighteenth century built four houses in Henrietta Street, Dublin, one as his residence, the others as speculation, before his appointment as Ranger of the Phoenix Park. There he designed and built for himself a house which was to become the Viceregal Lodge, and finally Áras an Uachtaráin. About 1770 he decided to move into the country, adjacent to the city, and on 471 acres at Killadoon on the river Liffey near Celbridge, he built a fine mansion, which he never saw to completion. His son Robert was created Earl of Leitrim in 1795, that being their ancestral county, the Clements having settled there in the early seventeenth century.

During the agrarian troubles of 1795, when Killadoon was raided in the absence of the family, Lord Clare communicated to Nathaniel, Lord Clements, the eldest son of the earl of Leitrim, that: 'On Saturday night some of the most forward Assertors of the Cause paid a visit to Killadoon where they displayed the true principles of fraternity in taking to themselves whatever they found which the proprietor seemed not to have immediate occasion for. Arms and horses were the principal Booty there; I hope your hunters were not at grass…'

Three years later Killadoon was again raided, and before the battle of nearby Ovidstown in May 1798 a group of insurgents entered the estate and took some of the servants as prisoners. One of the servants, armed with a bayonet, obstructed the rebels at the door of

*Killadoon*

the house and swore that he would have the life of any man that entered, and he wounded two of them before being taken prisoner. Then the rebels drove cattle off the estate to feed their army.

Killadoon survived the outrages of that time, and in 1800 when Nathaniel, Lord Clements, married Mary Bermingham from Galway they honeymooned there, before returning to Lisburn where he was colonel of his regiment, the Donegal militia. He succeeded to the title of 2nd Earl of Leitrim in 1804, and they came to live at Killadoon where he soon set about improving the house and the estate.

In keeping with his new statues he purchased 'a new fashionable town coach, made with projecting elbows and round sides, compas'd pillars and roof rails, painted yellow, a sword case in the back, lined with fine cloth in the Improved manner, a Perth carriage and hooptire wheels.' The total cost of the coach was £386.16.6 including such extras as 'a Salisbury boot fixed on blocks, Japanned and polished and plated mouldings and steps, in lieu of the coach box and platform at £12, and a scarlet hammer cloth trimmed with silk and worsted lace, and two rows of deep fringe with silk hangers and a broad stripe of black velvet at £23. Venetian blinds to the windows cost £3.13.0 and a pair of hanging pieces with crest and coronet £1.4.0. Painting the Arms and Supporters on the door, and crest and coronet on the quarter panels, cost £7.14.0.' It must have been a splendid sight, and when his lordship drove into Dublin there were always four horses and two postillions. And he did not neglect her ladyship: other household expenses included 'shoes for Lady Clements £1.3.0. for two pairs of grey kid shoes, 11/6 for a purple pair, and £1.8.0 for two pairs of purple Roman boots.'

Lady Leitrim spent much of her time with her children, of whom she had eleven, five sons and six daughters: 'they are seldom away from me, I draw, I play the piano forte, I go through all my studies regularly; I never walk out but with the children.' The children played in the ornamental thatched cottage, which had been built some thirty years before as a retreat for the ladies. Decorated with a rustic porch and coloured glass, including two panes painted by the Duchess of Leinster, it was a very special place for them. In time, as was customary, the boys of the family were educated in England.

New stables were built at Killadoon in 1814; there were to be 15 stalls, and six coach horses. That autumn Elizabeth Clements wrote to her absent father: 'the stables go on very well, we go to see them every day that we may send you the account ... the places for the mangers are finished in both the stables and for the grate in the coach house'. Then she described a hare hunt in which three hares were sprung and one killed. Another diversion, which she wrote about, was the visit of the dancing master Mr O'Brien: 'we dance *Pas de Deux* at the four corners of the room.'

In the summer time the children went to visit their aunt, Lady Charlemont, (née Anne Bermingham of Rose Hill, county Galway) at Marino, Dublin, and sometimes there were other outings, such as that in June 1817 to the Phoenix Park: 'yesterday after the laying of the first stone of the Wellington testimonial when all the gentlemen and ladies were gone to the Lodge, some ladies danced a quadrilla on the grass, although there had been several showers in the morning and the grass was quite wet. The Lord Lieutenant had a white satin apron, trimmed with gold fringe, a silver trowel, a gild hammer, and two gild squares, to try if the stone was at right angles.... all the ladies had branches of laurel, and aunt Charlemont brought home hers.'

But there were also difficult times at Killadoon, such as in 1820 when famine afflicted the west of Ireland and the tenants were unable to pay their rents. The Leitrims went to Paris to economise. From there Leitrim wrote to his agent at home: 'I am sorry to tell you I have been obliged to draw upon Coutts already, and that he is now in advance of £600.' Soon after in another letter he explained: 'Were my children younger the plan for me to pursue would be very simple; to go to Ireland and live quietly there in the hope of better times; but with a large family like mine (there were then eight children), just entering life, to take them to Ireland now, considering the state to which poor Ireland is reduced, and the utter impossibility under which I should be of having any society for them at Killadoon, would be complete ruin to any views that I might form of marrying my daughters and settling them with advantage in the world. What chance would they have now of marrying with any degree of advantage in Ireland? To take them to Killadoon at present would be only making a second edition of what old Watson used to call the Nunnery; and recollect that if they should not marry, I cannot possibly provide for them as my father did for my two sisters.... I have not been influenced by any selfish motive; in fact if I was so influenced, I should return immediately to Killadoon, for neither Lady Leitrim nor I ever enjoy ourselves anywhere else as much as we do there, certainly not in London.'

A decade later Leitrim was in a more expansive mood when he wrote to his eldest son, Lord Clements, giving the expenses he had incurred in outfitting himself and his lady for the coronation of William IV. After attending the coronation of Queen Victoria in 1838 Lady Leitrim told her son William, '…poor Lord Rolle fell when trying to get to the foot of the throne to do homage. The queen sent Lord Conyngham to assist him, which with the aid of other peers, he at length succeeded in accomplishing; when he reached the foot of the throne the queen rose immediately and stepped forward in the most graceful and the most gracious manner, to present her hand and crown, that Lord Rolle might do homage, without the fatigue and exertion of ascending the steps of the throne. Later, when the Duke of Wellington did homage in the Abbey, he was immediately cheered more even than the queen herself. The duke gave a ball to celebrate the coronation.'

But if the coronation celebrations brought happiness to the Clements family, there was also sorrow. In 1837 George, a naval officer, had died of yellow fever in Sierra Leone, and two years afterwards there was further sadness when Robert, the eldest son, died unmarried at the age of thirty-four, while his parents were abroad. It was his death, which led to the succession of his brother, William Sydney, as the ill-fated 3rd Earl of Leitrim.

Lady Leitrim died in 1840, and the earl remarried and fathered three more daughters, bringing his total progeny to fourteen. The 2nd Earl's six daughters of the first marriage all married, but he was not so fortunate with his five sons, only one of whom wed. In his will the Earl had bequeathed to his heir Robert Lord Clements:

'all the furniture, books, linen, china, glass and everything else belonging to my house at Killadoon (and with respect to my books my wish is that all my books relating to Irish history and Irish affairs in general should, as far as Law allows it, descend as an heir-loom for ever to the person inheriting the title of Leitrim) with the exception of my portrait and bust, the former painted by Sir Thomas Lawrence and the latter executed by Nollekens, both of which I leave my beloved wife for her life, and after her decease to my son above mentioned. I likewise leave him all the gardening and farming utensils at Killadoon, and stock of every kind whether live or dead; and if I should die before he is of age I request that during his minority my beloved wife will make it her residence, by which I do not mean to preclude her from going to England or any other place that may be of advantage to herself or of my children – my meaning is that she should have the same enjoyment of the house and place during my son's minority that she had in my lifetime; and my wish is that the house and place should be kept up (at my son's expense) in the same manner that I have kept it up, and as my beloved wife is acquainted with my various plans of improvement my anxious wish is that they should as far as possible (and I trust that the Court of Chancery will confirm these wishes) lay out any sum of money arising from my son's income during his minority which in her opinion may contribute to the improvement of the place and tend to attach my son to it hereafter. And I further charge her to sell or exchange any of the furniture or anything else belonging to Killadoon which from wear and tear, change of fashion or any other cause it may be desirable to part with as I have the fullest confidence in her judgement. I am perfectly convinced that in every act my dear son's interest will be her first object. I further give and bequeath to my dear son Robert Birmingham Lord Clements, after the decease of my beloved wife, the above mentioned Estate held under the University of Dublin (subject to certain annuities and charges as will be mentioned hereafter) and all my plate which is not entailed, and in case he should died before he is of age my Will is that these bequests should go to my second son William Sydney Clements.'

On the death of his father in 1854 William Sydney succeeded to the title. He had graduated from Sandhurst and, with his younger brother Charles, served in Portugal in the 1820s. William, after he returned home with the rank of lieutenant colonel, was Aide de Camp to the Lord Lieutenant in Dublin, and Charles was also an ADC, to the Governor General of Canada. Of the two other sons, George was a naval captain, and Francis a clergyman.

The 3rd Earl of Leitrim, at the age of seventy-two, was murdered on 2nd April 1878. It was not the first time that he had been ambushed: on 18 April 1857 he noted in his diary that when he was travelling to Killadoon 'I was shot at passing through Tooman. Two copper caps snapped. The gun or pistol misfired. I went to the house of the widow Burbage and her son Mch'l Burbage appeared to be the person who had done the act.'

Leitrim had a record of the harsh treatment and evicting of tenants. In March 1867 he wrote in his diary: 'Gave directions that Thos. O'Neill should be dismissed in consequence of his having allowed a priest, O'Bierne, to hold a station in my house occupied by him as my servant, and making use of it to obtain an opposition to Noble's election to the Poor Law Guardians.'

In January 1870 there was a robbery at Killadoon, as noted in Leitrim's diary: 'two shirts, two pocket handkerchiefs were taken out of the Bleach Green, and some lemons taken from the Green House & some of the gardener's tools. Went to the garden and examined the footmarks of the man who had been there on Monday night. I took a model of them and compared with Rutherford's and remarked his mode of walking which left no doubt of his being the man.'

That Leitrim's bad reputation had by then reached the highest authority is evident from this diary entry: 'had a long conversation with the Chief Secretary at the Park, (in the house built by his great-grandfather Nathaniel Clements). He appeared at first inclined to give me trouble, and talked about the harsh way in which I treated my tenants. I told him that it was false. I asked him to remove Hill, the County Inspector for Donegal.'

When the Earl was murdered in County Donegal, his clerk and his carman were also killed in an outrage which was seen as a prelude to the Land War. Leitrim was brought home to Killadoon to be waked before removal by train to Kingsbridge for burial in the vaults of St Michan's Church, Dublin. The arrival of the cortège at Kingsbridge coincided with the departure of a train to Naas with punters bound for the Punchestown races. The high spirits of some of the crowd led to the venting of their anger against the unpopular departed Earl, and the chasing of the galloping hearse over the cobbles to Church Street, where the churchyard gates were hurriedly locked to prevent further desecration.

In 1960 a plaque was erected at the place of the assassination, but not to the Earl of Leitrim: the inscription remembers the three perpetrators 'who by their heroism at Cratlagh Wood on 2 April 1878, ended the tyranny of landlordism in Ireland.' That murder forms the kernel of Brian Friel's play *The Home Place* which was premiered at the Abbey theatre in recent times. Leitrim was succeeded as 4th Earl by his nephew, the eldest son of the Revd Francis Clements, Vicar of Norton. His son, the 5th and last Earl, though twice married, died without issue, and as his younger brother and heir presumptive, Francis Patrick Clements RN, had disappeared without trace in 1906, the peerage became extinct.

In 1991 Lt Col. Charles Marcus Lefevre Clements, as President of the *County Kildare Archaeological Society,* led members of that society to the vault at St Michan's and there gave a talk on the life and death of his grand-uncle the 3rd Earl of Leitrim, ironically now the most widely remembered member of a distinguished family.

Col. Clements himself served with the Queen's Hussars in India, where he was a champion at pig sticking. During the Second World War he was serving in Germany when he was captured in 1941, having already been awarded the Military Cross for his service in the campaign in Greece. During his time in the prisoner of war camp he was head of the escape committee, and when he was released in 1945 he managed to get home in time for Punchestown races! Back with his regiment, he was given command of the POW camp for German generals in Wales, and in 1948 he accompanied Field Marshal von Runsted back to Germany.

The third and youngest brother, Robin, was a strong nationalist. He spent three years of the Second World War in the internment camp for Republicans on the Curragh, and as a fluent Irish speaker, he taught the language to his fellow prisoners. Robin was also a keen railway enthusiast, and a journey to Cork or Limerick with the driver on the locomotive engine was for him a happy excursion.

Henry and Charles Clements, and their sister Kitty, (whose grandfather Col. Henry Theophilus Clements was listed in the *Curragh Directory* of 1887) were enthusiastic members of the Kildare Hunt Club. Charles was Honorary Secretary and later President of the

*Lt Col. Henry Theophilus Wickham Clements 1898-1974*

hunt, while Kitty continued to hunt until she was almost ninety years of age. She and her brothers were believed to have inspired novelist Aidan Higgins, a neighbour at Celbridge, when he was writing *Langrish, Go Down*, the story of the demise of an Anglo-Irish gentry family in the years between the two world wars. Henry Clements served in both world wars, and died unmarried in 1974. He bequeathed the family estate of Lough Rynne to his cousin Marcus, and Killadoon to his sister Kitty for life, with remainder to Marcus's son Charles.

The Clements family still occupies Killadoon, though much of the 487-acre estate there has been consumed by development.

## Wolfes of Forenaghts

When Maud Wolfe died in 1980 the three hundred year connection of her family with County Kildare ended. Unmarried, she had lived at Forenaughts, Naas, for seventy years, having moved there with her parents from Bishopland, Ballymore Eustace, when she was eighteen. In 1908 the estates of Forenaughts and Bishopsland totalled 1,397 acres, and the status of the family is evident in that a section of the graveyard at Ballymore Eustace was reserved for the Wolfes.

Maud's father, George Wolfe, had served in the Royal Irish Fusiliers and taken part in the battle of Telel- Kebir, before settling into the life style of a county gentleman, and a member of Kildare County Council from its formation in 1899 to 1932, as well as representing the County in Dáil Éireann from 1923 to 1932. He studied the Irish language, and in 1914 he was present at the review of the National Volunteers at the Gibbet Rath on the Curragh. His active participation in local affairs included being a founder member of the *County Kildare Archaeological Society,* and president of the society in 1932. He was a Peace Commissioner, and Ranger of the Curragh, until his death in 1941. Maud was a member of the council of the *Kildare Archaeological Society* for thirty-seven years.

The Wolfe family of Forenaughts was connected to another prominent County Kildare family through the marriage in 1753 of Capt. Philpott Wolfe, Kildare Militia, JP and High Sheriff, to Mary Burgh, a grand-niece of Surveyor General Thomas Burgh of Oldtown, Naas. In the summer of 1783 their eldest son, Captain John Wolfe, commanded a squadron in the review of Volunteers, which was said to have attracted 50,000 spectators to the Curragh, and later he was colonel of the Yeomanry unit, the Forenaughts Cavalry.

*The Wolfe family crest, which depicts the heads of wolves*

Well might Sir Bernard Burke say in his *Landed Gentry*, 'This family is of great antiquity, and has not been undistinguished.' Distinguished members included Maj. Gen. James Wolfe, the hero of Quebec, and Lt Richard Wolfe, Scots Greys, who at the age of twenty-nine, was killed in the attempt in 1885 to relieve General Gordon in the Sudan.

Parson Charles Wolfe is remembered as the author of *The burial of Sir John Moore at Corunna* (in 1809). He was the eight son of Thomas Wolfe of Blackhall, Clane. When he was ordained in 1817 and appointed to a remote parish in County Tyrone just before Christmas of that year, he revealed the loneliness of his mission: 'I am sitting by myself opposite my turf fire with my bible beside me in the only furnished room of the glebe house, surrounded by mountains, frost, snow, and by a set of people with whom I am totally unacquainted, except for a disbanded artillery man and his wife and two children who attend me as church warden and clerk of the parish.'

Wolfe loved Irish music and put words to some of the tunes. 'Irish music,' he believed 'often gives us the idea of a mournful retrospect upon our gaiety, which cannot help catching a little of the spirit of that very gaiety which it's lamenting.' When he died at the age of thirty-one his doctor said that 'It was remarkable to see such a mind in a body so wasted, there was something supernatural about that man.'

His first cousin, Arthur Wolfe, Viscount Kilwarden and Lord Chief Justice, was the eighth of the nine sons of John Wolfe of Forenaughts. In 1798 Kilwarden had unsuccessfully endeavoured to save Wolfe Tone from the gallows. Tone's family lived at Bodenstown, as tenants of the Wolfe family of Blackhall. Tone himself was named after his godfather Theobald Wolfe, a distinguished barrister, and it was said that his mother was a companion to Mrs Wolfe of Blackhall.

Lord Kilwarden, with his nephew Revd Richard Straubengie Wolfe, was murdered in Dublin during the Emmet rebellion of 1803. Fortunately, Kilwarden's daughter Marianne was rescued from the mêlée and given shelter in a house nearby.

Sir Jonah Barrington, the judge and historian from Abbeyleix, expressed his opinion of Kilwarden: 'On first acquaintance Kilwarden seldom failed to make an unfavourable impression, but his arrogance was only apparent, his pride innoxious, his haughtiness theoretical. In society he so whimsically mixed and mingled solemn ostentation with playful frivolity, that the man and the boy, the judge and the jester were generally alternate.'

George Wolfe of Forenaughts, a member of the Naas Board of Guardians in 1849, who had been nominated to arrange 'the sending of emigrant paupers from Naas Union to the Canadas,' reported to the board '300 emigrant paupers from Naas Union sailed from Dublin to Quebec...the emigrants left Dublin with an excellent outfit, a very liberal supply of excellent provisions.' It was also noted that Mr Wolfe had given each adult £1, and children under fourteen 10/-, 'to assist them up the country when they arrived in Quebec.'

The Wolfes were connected to the Hendrick family of Tully, Kildare, and Kerdiffstown, Naas, through the marriage of Mary, the only daughter of Thomas Wolfe of Blackhall, in 1758 to Charles Hendrick. He was the son of a Dublin brewer, on the site of whose establishment the Guinness brewery was later built. Members of the Hendrick family also married into the Borrowes, de Burgh and Aylmer families, and in 1889 the Kerdiffstown estates passed to Hans Hendrick Aylmer, the son of Michael Aylmer of Courtown.

It was a popular perception of the Wolfes that 'although sprung from Norman stock, it could in truth be said that they were more Irish than the Irish themselves.'

Top left: *Hans Hendrick Aylmer*

Top right: *Arthur Wolfe, first Viscount Kilwarden*

Above left: *Wolfe Tone*

Above right: *George Wolfe of Forenaughts*

Right: *Revd Charles Wolfe*

## Weldons of Kilmorony

A family prominent in County Kildare, and in the neighbouring Queen's County, for three hundred years was that of Weldon, whose principal seats were at Rahinderry in the latter county, and at Kilmorony near Athy, where in 1883 they had in total 2,739 acres. Men of the family represented Athy in parliament; they were county High Sheriffs and Justices of the Peace, and entered holy orders or joined the army. Perhaps they might be taken as typical of many ascendancy families who traced their origins from English adventurers who sought land and wealth in Ireland in the disturbed years of the sixteenth and seventeenth centuries.

Walter Weldon was one of four brothers who acquired estates in the midlands, and in 1613 he was a Member of Parliament, and resident at St John's Bower, Athy. As the Weldons settled and flourished in their new homes they intermarried with families of a similar background, and they set about the improvement of their estates and the building of their fine houses. Even if they never achieved the respect of their native neighbours to the extent that the banished landowners had, and there were no ties of race or religion, the Weldons and their class did occupy the most important roles in the society of their times.

The *Military Directory* of 1887 lists Sir Anthony Weldon Baronet, of Kilmorony, Athy. He was one of a family which produced many military men who gave distinguished service to the British Empire. A modern study of the family shows that from the mid-eighteenth century seventeen men followed the colours in the Indian or British army, one of whom reached the rank of major-general in the Madras artillery, and another that of Surveyor General of Egypt in the years of the Great War. Weldons fell in the Boer War and the two Great Wars.

At a soldier's sing-song in Athy Town Hall in April 1915 Mrs Weldon encouraged 'all young men to go and help their fellow countrymen. Athy, out of a population of 4,000 had sent 300 men, and if other towns did as well the war would soon be over.... the example of the Leinsters and Dublin Fusiliers should inspire the young men to go and do their part for their King and Country.'

At one period during the Great War there were no less than twelve Weldons at the Front simultaneously. At home in Kilmorony Mrs Weldon, having felt anxious for several days, thought she heard a voice calling her on the day before news came of the death of one of her sons. But she did not fail in her duty at home and organised the local *Comfort Fund for Soldiers at the Front,* as well as arranging entertainments for the men based in her own locality.

*Captain George Weldon, R.D.F. who was killed in South Africa in 1899*

Lt Col. Anthony Weldon, who had been in charge of troops in the Limerick/Clare area in 1916, died the following year in action in France. The obituaries in the county Kildare papers described him as 'being popular with all classes, an indulgent landlord, and a keen sportsman.' Of his service in Limerick in 1916 it was said that he availed of the situation there to study 'the psychology of the revolutionary movement. The most unkind word he could find in his heart to say of them was that they were misguided. He did not say they were knaves, rogues or traitors, merely from his point of view they were misguided'.

The ending of the Great War did not bring peace to Ireland, and when a truce was declared in the Anglo-Irish war it was not observed in Athy. During a raid by thirty disguised men on the home of the widowed Lady Weldon, in which field glasses and other items were taken, Lady Weldon protested her patriotism. A public remonstrance was made to Sinn Fein following that outrage.

The findings of a modern study by *FÁS* of the family were that 'after 300 years of residence in Ireland the Weldons were forced, like so many other Anglo-Irish landed gentry, to retreat to England leaving behind a chequered family history, with only the ruins of their dwellings, memorials to their war heroes, and gravestones as a reminder of their presence in Ireland.' This was a sad conclusion to a family saga, but one which could describe the fate of countless families of all classes.

## Barton of Straffan

Not too far from Killadoon is the nineteenth century Italianate and French château style Straffan House, built by Hugh Barton, the grandson of Thomas Barton from County Fermanagh who had established himself in the wine business in Bordeaux in 1725. During the reign of terror in France, from 1793 to 1794, many of the big merchants were imprisoned and, as an alien, Hugh Barton was apprehended. However, with the assistance of his Bordeaux-born wife he escaped and came to Ireland, bringing mementoes of his adventures which he gave to a museum in Dublin, but which are now lost.

ANCIENT MOTTO:-

VIS FORTIBUS ARMA

*The Barton family crest*

As he was forbidden to hold property in France, Barton arranged for his partner, Daniel Guestier, to take over and manage his business there. This agreement, informal though it was, lasted well into the nineteenth century, when it was formalised. Ever since then descendants of Barton and Guestier have managed their extensive vineyards, and the label *B & G* is firmly established in the wine market. When it was prudent to return to France, Hugh resumed his business there, and in 1822 he purchased the Chateau Leoville, where his descendants still live, and Chateau Langoa, in St Julien. Barton, who was High Sheriff of County Kildare in 1840, built the house, at Straffan, and he retained the stables of an older house on the site. Later he also built the Protestant church in the village. His grandson, Col. H.L. Barton, High Sheriff, was listed in the *Curragh Directory* of 1887.

From Hugh was also descended the Barton family of Glendalough where his third son, Thomas Johnston, lived at Glendalough House. Thomas's son Charles married Agnes Childers in 1918, and her half-brother Robert Childers, a great orientalist, married her sister-in-law Anna Maria Barton. Their grandson was the late President Erskine Childers. Another prominent member of the Glendalough family was Robert Childers Barton. A supporter of Sinn Fein, he was a member of the party which went to London to negotiate the Anglo-Irish Treaty in 1921. He represented Counties Kildare and Wicklow in Dáil Éireann, and was Minister for Agriculture in the first years of the State.

Derick Barton was the last member of the family to live at Straffan, and he published his *Memories of Ninety Years* in 1991. In it he recalled his half-century of life at Straffan, as well as his service in both the Irish and British armies during the Second World War. Observing the demise of the once almost feudal landed class to which for a time he belonged, he quipped: 'A friend suggested I entitle these memoirs *From Castle to Cottage,*' a proposal he dismissed as he had not come from a castle, and he was then living in an apartment in Dublin.

His tolerance of change, and acceptance of the new order, was remarkable. From a childhood spent partly in France, and in a happy home staffed with numerous servants, and attended by their private chaplain, he went to Eton and Sandhurst. Before the Great War, he recalled, 'with the army still in occupation on the Curragh, in Kildare and in Newbridge, there was an enormous following of the Kildare hunt and it has always remained a vivid picture in my mind, these seventy years later. There was generally a guest or two from the garrisons at the Curragh or Newbridge staying at Straffan. I am not sure if their horses came with them, there was ample room in the stables, and for the soldier grooms in the rooms overhead, or they may have come by train to Straffan Station next morning.'

Derick returned home from Sandhurst to serve in the army in Buttevant and Galway during the final days of the British era when horses, hunting, tennis and socialising almost disguised the undercurrent of violence throughout the country. In a tranquil valley in Connemara he and a comrade were fortunate to survive a shooting, and some time later, returning in a taxi from the cinema, one of his companions was shot dead. In his remembrance of that time he commented on 'the involvement of his rebel cousin Robert Barton of Glendalough... who was on De Valera's team.'

Army life in England he found was less dangerous, and he was fortunate to be chosen to participate in the Pentathlon championships at the Paris Olympics of 1924. The death of his father in a hunting accident, shortly after the birth of Derick's son in 1927, required him to leave the army and take over the management of Straffan.

There he found the estate was not economically viable, but he immersed himself in the task of sustaining it. An active member of the Farmers' Union, he was nominated by the farmers' party in the general election, when he got 4,000 votes, but was not elected.

*Straffan House, home of the Henry and Barton families*

Chairman of the Kildare Hunt Club, he recalled that the annual Hunt Ball in Naas Town Hall was for him an important annual social occasion, and he structurally altered his own house to enable dances to be held there. He also enjoyed tennis at the County Club in Naas, remembering that as a boy he had played cricket there. But he was also interested in politics, and his membership of the Blue Shirts and Fine Gael, led to his appearing before a military court, and being arrested again on another occasion.

During the Emergency he joined the Officers' Training Corps at the Curragh, one of the few gentlemen of the landed class to serve in the Irish army. He had some good tales to tell about his service in Waterford, New Ross, Kilkenny and the Curragh, and of a Christmas dinner celebrated with his family in a Newbridge hotel. Other stories he enjoyed telling included those of the involvement of the army in the control of the foot and mouth disease. Barton recalled the bombing at Campile, County Wexford in 1940, and in the following year, when bombs fell on the Curragh plains. But his most unusual experience was in Kilkenny when, as Orderly Officer, he was not recognised by a sentry, a new recruit, and was marched across the barrack square with a rifle to his back!

After a time he decided to go to Britain and re-enlist there, where he was employed on administrative duties, and later in a German POW camp.

Back in Straffan in 1947 he resumed farming, but as he concedes himself 'perhaps I was not meant to be a farmer.' In the 1960s he sold what was left of the estate and moved to Dublin. There he became president of the Royal Dublin Society and for several years filled the position with distinction.

Derick Barton's reminiscences are of interest as they describe County life during a most crucial period in our history, and when the motivation, loyalties and ambitions of Barton's world were indelibly altered. As Kitty Clements of Killadoon had remarked of Straffan and its big indoor staff in Derick's fathers day; 'All those footmen, it was like Buckingham Palace.'

Straffan is now again comparable to a palace, having been transformed into a first class hotel, with a golf course on which major international competitions are held.

## Medlicotts of Dunmurray

The English family of Medlicott is first recorded in this county in the early eighteenth century when George Medlicott of Tully purchased the estate of Youngstown and Dunmurray; subsequently they also occupied lands at Ardscull, Moortown and Ballysax.

However, their ascendancy was not necessarily welcomed, and in the Autumn of 1707 the burgesses of the corporation of Kildare presented a petition to the House of Commons complaining 'of several practices of George Medlicott and his sons, in procuring themselves to be elected sovereigns of the borough of Kildare for several years successively, and in making great numbers of freemen, on condition that they should vote for magistrates and burgesses of parliament, as the said Mr Medlicott and his sons should direct.'

From early in the eighteenth century they regularly held the office of Sovereign of the corporation of Kildare town, an office that included the exercising of control over the Curragh plain, and the protection of the grazing-rights there. In 1836 when the Kildare Grand Jury proposed striking a rate in respect of the plain on the landowners fronting the sward, and so to raise a salary for the Conservator of the Curragh, to which office Graydon Medlicott had been appointed, some of the local gentlemen objected, and the Office of Woods and Forests which controlled the Curragh had the innovation suppressed.

It is interesting to find that in 1866 when a commission was taking evidence of the status of the plain and a witness was telling of the nuisance of *foreigners* (unauthorised sheep) he praised Mr Medlicott, saying that 'when he was sovereign of Kildare he took management of the Curragh into his own hands. The sheep belonging to the farmers who had not paid the Curragh cess were driven off and sold, but this practice ceased about 1830.'

As with many of the County families, the younger Medlicotts often went into the services and holy orders, and the daughters sometimes married clergymen. The Revd Samuel Medlicott (1796-1858), rector of Loughrea, County Galway, was the youngest of four sons, and his youngest son was also in orders. His two eldest sons went to India where one of them became the director of the Geological Survey of India.

The Revd Samuel is remembered in folk history. He had a housekeeper named Brídín Vesey, a daughter of the parish clerk in Loughrea. She was very friendly with the poet Antoine Ó Reachtabhra (Blind Raftery), and when Parson Medlicott was transferred to Killaloe she accompanied him, and the poet was heartbroken. In his grief he wrote one of the most beautiful love songs in the Irish language, *Brídín Vesey.*

J. E. Medlicott of Dunmurry House, Kildare, was amongst the county gentlemen listed in the *Military Directory* of 1887. Nowadays the Medlicotts, who once occupied 1,500 acres of land and for two hundred years held many positions of responsibility in the county, and who gave many notable men to the church and the British Colonial Service, are no longer represented here. With the sale of Dunmurray in 1955 the family's connection with this county ceased. An impressive vault in the grounds of St Brigid's Cathedral, Kildare, is their resting place.

# 8

# New Arrivals

## Conolly of Castletown

'**M**any people here, especially our quality and old gentry, are much offended at Mr Conolly's being one of them; this gentleman was lately an attorney, his father keeping an ale-house in the north of Ireland, this being too notorious to be stifled, but by making long bills and good bargains, he is now reported to be worth eight thousand a year, and by a generous way of living and adhering to the honest cause in bad times, was chosen Speaker of the House of Commons this parliament, but has shown himself very unequal to that part, but has still a considerable interest in the House, and gave his assistance to the late Justices in this last Session.' So wrote Sir John St Leger, Baron of the Exchequer in Ireland, to Chief Justice Parker in February 1717 of William Conolly, Speaker of the Irish House of Commons.

That candid opinion of a new arrival on the social and political scene must be such as has been uttered many times before, and since! The St Legers themselves had arrived under the auspices of King Henry VIII, and in 1542 had been granted the Nunnery of Graney, Castledermot, and other lands: as Hiram Morgan has commented 'profiteering from dissolved monastic and confiscated rebel lands by way of speculation and under valuation.'

Now the St Legers are gone from the county, but the Conollys, represented by Lord Carew, have left a magnificent legacy in their great classical house at Castletown, Celbridge, with its associated follies. The 45 metre obelisk, known as Conolly's Folly, the Temple and the Wonderful Barn, all visible from Castletown, were erected by the Speaker's widow to provide local employment during the famine of 1740/41. With the house, they are today state-owned heritage property.

Despite his humble origin Speaker Conolly had married into the ascendancy Conyngham family from his home county of Donegal, and when he died in 1729, the house passed to his nephew, another William. William's wife, Lady Anne Conolly, was a daughter of Thomas Wentworth, Earl of Strafford., who had built the great Jigginstown House at Naas in the seventeenth century. When William died just two years later, Castletown passed to his nephew Thomas Conolly, the richest commoner in the country, who at the age of twenty married Lady Louisa Augusta Lennox, a daughter of the duke of Richmond.

Tom Conolly is remembered in the annals of foxhunting in County Kildare as 'a fine sporting gentleman, amongst the first to maintain a private hunting establishment,' and as 'the greatest figure in the history of eighteenth century horse racing and breeding in Ireland.' He purchased the lease of a house in Kildare town to be near the Curragh, and 'he became virtually the father of the Turf Club.' But he also found time for social

*Thomas Conolly, who died in 1803*

involvement, and both he and Louisa were governors of the Kildare Infirmary. When Tom Conolly died in 1803 his widow had an elaborate monument erected in his memory in the old church at Kildrought. In recent times it has been moved to Castletown House.

Conolly's sister Jane had eloped with George Robert 'Fighting' FitzGerald from Mayo. As she had a considerable fortune, for some years they lived splendidly and expensively in Paris until forced to borrow from the suitably named Major Baggs. That arrangement ended in a duel, and though injured FitzGerald fled.

Such erratic behaviour alarmed his wife and she left him, and he returned to Mayo. There he was soon again in very serious trouble when he arranged the murder of a neighbour. Condemned to death at the Grand Assizes in 1786, he appeared on the scaffold dressed in 'a ragged coat of the Castletown hunt.' His body was brought home to be waked, but it was found that the house had been sacked, and the candles had to be stuck in bottles around his corpse. 'Fighting' FitzGerald was subsequently described in a pamphlet as 'an undutiful son, a bad brother, and a worse husband.'

Lady Louisa Conolly, with her sisters, Emily, Duchess of Leinster at nearby Carton, and Lady Sarah Napier at Oakley Park, Celbridge, had a happy and interesting life, the story of which has already been well told. And it was from Castletown that Lady Louisa, aunt of Lord Edward FitzGerald, set out one fine evening in 1798 to follow the bier of her ill-starred kinsman from the prison cell to his last resting place at St Werburgh's Church, Dublin. No other relative of the dead patriot was present.

Lady Isabella FitzGerald also recalled, 'speaking of the friends and companions of other times, I must not omit our agreeable neighbours, Louisa, and Emily Napier. These two charming sisters were, one the stepdaughter, and the other the daughter of my father's aunt Lady Sarah Napier. She had besides many boys, fine, spirited and clever boys (including the later General Sir George, conqueror of Scinde and General Sir William, historian of the Peninsular War) who with us were partakers of all the festivities of Castletown, where Lady Louisa and Mr Conolly, who had no children, delighted in being surrounded by us all. How delightful were the hours, which we passed there, in Emily's beautiful conservatory, for she was the adopted child of Lady Louisa. Sweet were our walks through the woods....by the banks of the Liffey, which unlike our peaceful Rye water at Carton runs its rapid course over large stones and rocks, which perhaps we might have viewed with envy had not the river at Carton, at this time, afforded us the pleasure of boating a great deal, which always make a variety in a country life.'

When Lady Louisa died at Castletown in 1821, sitting in a tent before her house, as she had wished, there was no male heir. Col. Edward Pakenham of the Longford family, a grandson of Thomas Conolly's sister, inherited the estate of 2,600 acres and he assumed the name and arms of Conolly. He died in 1848. His heir, also named Thomas (1823–1876), was in America during the Civil War and his diary of his adventures there has been published.

But his adventurous life had led to financial difficulties, and he found it necessary to sell off a portion of his property. At the age of forty-five he married a rich neighbour's daughter, Miss Sarah Eliza Shaw of Temple House, Celbridge. Their nuptials were celebrated at his agent's Parsonstown House, near Castletown, with 'upwards of a hundred of the tenantry of the home estate of Mr Conolly together with a host of other respectable inhabitants in the vicinity of Celbridge and its neighbourhood, with viands in profusion and the eatables faultless.' The *Irish Times* reporter, who enjoyed the feast, wrote that he had seldom seen 'a finer well dressed more warm-hearted tenantry than those who came to pay their respects and offer their felicitations to the popular couple.'

Soon after their marriage the Conollys were in Paris where they 'became a familiar sight, vying in good-natured competition with Tom's friend, Napoleon III, to see whose carriage was more splendidly turned out (Conolly won; his horses were shod in silver).' In a short time, the Conolly succession seemed assured with the birth of another Thomas in 1870.

Eight years later Tom Conolly was dead, leaving three sons and a daughter. A glimpse of his life-style was given in a tribute by Lady St Helier: 'His hospitality was unbounded, and his house was always full. There were horses to ride, there were cars to be driven; there was an excellent cook and plenty of champagne. Dear old Tom Conolly! He was the kindest, the brightest, the most delightful of people, perfect as a host, a kind and staunch friend and universally beloved'. The *Irish Times* agreed with those sentiments, adding that Conolly was 'genial, kindly, generous to a fault, patriotic in sentiment, where the best interests of Ireland were concerned, and one of the very best of our resident landlords.'

Constantia Maxwell, the historian of the Georgian years, had this impression of the gentry: 'The first thing that struck the English traveller in Ireland in the eighteenth century was the extravagant way of living of the Irish gentry, their extraordinary hospitality and the conviviality of their manners.' However, she did not include the master of Castletown in that category: 'There were people in Ireland, however, who could be hospitable without being vulgar, the Right Hon. Thomas Conolly of Castletown, for instance, son (sic) (He was a grand-nephew) of the famous Speaker of the Irish House of Commons, who was one of the richest landowners in the country. The diarist Mrs Delany remembered the hospitality of Mrs Conolly, the widow of the Speaker, who had as regular a life as a member of the French court.'

Conolly's brother, John Augustus, who had merited a Victoria Cross in the Crimea, was Resident Magistrate in the Curragh in 1887 when he was listed as one of the guests at a ball in the camp gymnasium. It was a very grand affair as the attendance included the Prince and Princess Edward of Saxe-Weimar and numerous high-ranking officers. Other members of County families who enjoyed the occasion included de Robecks, de Burghs, La Touches, Blackers and Moores.

Tom Conolly's successor at Castletown, his son Thomas, was killed while serving with the Scots Greys in South Africa in 1900, and his brother Major Edward Conolly succeeded him. He did not immediately settle at Castletown, and the house was sometimes rented. Lady Fingall encouraged Tom Kelly, 'a rich American and extreme Nationalist' who had rented Castletown, when owned by Maj. Conolly, to give a big Ball there. The Chief Secretary, George Wyndham (who was related to the FitzGeralds) and his party stayed at Castletown. Lady Fingall 'remembered fighting with Wyndham for the bath the next morning, and everyone came from Dublin and the country about, and even from the yachts anchored at Kingstown. I don't know what it cost, but we sent the invitations and Tom Kelly paid the bills!'

By 1922 Daisy Fingall's world was collapsing. Lord Mayo's Palmerstown had been burned, and one night 'they came to Castletown. They brought fifty gallons of petrol to burn the house, with its wonderful hall and the staircase that I remembered, where I had that vision of the ladies of another time going up to bed with their candlesticks, its Vandycks and Hogarths, and the portrait by Sir Joshua of Squire Tom Conolly; the vases with the eagle on them, given to a member of the family by Napoleon.....all these, and the great historical memories of Castletown, were to be laid on the smoking pyre of the new Ireland. Just before the petrol was thrown, a motorcycle came up the long avenue in a great hurry. And a breathless young man with some mysterious authority, (Art O'Connor of Sinn Fein, who had been elected to the First *Dáil Éireann* in 1919), rode into the middle of the group of burners, to say that on no account was the house to be touched that had been built with Irish money by William Conolly, who was Speaker of the Irish House of Commons two hundred years or so earlier.'

Christopher Hussey, writing in *Country Life* in 1936, said that 'Major E. M. Conolly, the present owner, puts into practice, as far as conditions admit, the hope expressed in his will by Squire Conolly, 'that the persons entitled to my estate will be resident in Ireland, and will always prove steady friends to Ireland, as their ancestor, Mr Speaker Conolly, the original and honest maker of my fortune, was.'

It is recalled locally in Celbridge that when Major Conolly died in 1956 the parish priest decreed that the staff were not to carry his coffin into the Protestant Church (at the entrance gate to Castletown), but they did. Some time later when one of the men was drunk on the main street of the town, he saw the priest and shouted at him 'The Major was the only man who ever gave us a day's work, why wouldn't we carry his coffin.'

The *Irish Times,* in the autumn of 1938, reported that 'Memories of past history in Ireland will be revived by the news that Lord and Lady Carew intend to live at Castletown. Lord Carew is a descendant of a great family, whose members were prominent in the Norman invasion. His mother was a daughter of the late Thomas Conolly MP of Castletown, County Kildare. Incidentally Castletown is one of the most historic homes in Ireland, and was the scene of many of the sporting adventures of the famous Squire Conolly. It was in one of the rooms there that the devil is said to have disappeared through a hearthstone when the parish priest at the squire's request debunked him. It used to be the custom to show sightseers the particular spot at which the Evil One disappeared. He had posed as a sportsman for the occasion, and had ridden to the hounds that day and beaten the squire!' Lord Carew inherited Castletown when Major Conolly died in 1956. His daughter, Diana Conolly-Carew, was on the Irish Team at the Olympic Games in 1968.

In 1965 the house and estate of 500 acres were sold for £166,000, and two years afterwards the Hon. Desmond Guinness purchased the house and 120 acres for £93,000. With his wife Mariga, and the newly founded *Irish Georgian Society,* the restoration of the house was commenced, and it was opened to the public.

*The Conolly Folly*

Consequently, when Mariga died in 1989 it was appropriate that she was buried beneath the Obelisk or Conolly's Folly, close to the great house which she had so enthusiastically sought to save. Castletown was acquired by *Dúchas, the Heritage Service* as a heritage property in 1994. Now, having been extensively conserved, the great house attracts a large number of visitors, while the concerts in the Long Gallery create an atmosphere compatible with its character.

## La Touche of Harristown

When John La Touche, of a Dublin Huguenot banking family, purchased in 1768 the old FitzEustace estate at Harristown, Kilcullen, he built himself a large house on high ground above the river Liffey, and set about enclosing his demesne. He diverted the road from Naas to Dunlavin with the construction of a new elegant bridge over the Liffey. Within sight of his house and within his park was the old bridge over the river and now, surrounded by mature beech trees, it remains a secret and tranquil place. There, one can imagine the young Rose La Touche walking with her tutor John Ruskin, and absorbing his philosophy. But that was in the mid-nineteenth century, when the building and planting of her great-grandfather had matured.

Col. Robert La Touche, MP for the rotten borough of Harristown, succeeded to the estate in 1822. He had raised the Kilcullen Yeomanry Cavalry, which in May 1798; he led to victory over the rebels at the ford on the river Liffey at Athgarvan.

His eldest son, John, was to be master of Harristown for sixty-two years, and with his formidable wife Maria Price, only child of the Dowager Countess of Desart, County Kilkenny, introduced many innovations to Harristown. John was High Sheriff of the County and Master of the Kildare Hunt. In the latter capacity he was 'prepared to keep the hounds for £300 a year.' With his brothers, Robert and William, John thoroughly enjoyed the chase, inspiring his wife to put his happiness in verse:

THE LA TOUCHE ARMS.

*The La Touche Arms*

His thoughts, if thoughts he have, have taken flight,
To some wild hunting country out of sight
In fancy listening to the much loved sounds,
Of horns, and trampling steeds, and baying hounds.

When Robert died suddenly in 1846 while attending the Curragh races, John resigned from the hunt and neither he nor his brother William ever hunted again. In the famine year of 1848 John gave employment to over 240 men on his 700-acre estate.

Being a fervent Christian and of evangelical convictions, which his wife did not always share, and living close to the Curragh Camp, John was disturbed by the immorality of many of the soldiers and of the *Wrens,* as the prostitutes who lived in the furze bushes on the plain were known. To awaken public interest in the problem in 1865 he gave a series of discourses in Naas Town Hall at which the attendance was 'sparse, but influential.' Explaining that he had been involved in evangelical work amongst 'the lost' in London, and was then on a committee in Dublin which managed a house for fallen women, he proposed that action should now be initiated locally to redeem the unfortunates. It was intended that ladies in the county would support a mission on behalf of the wretched class, 500 of whom it was calculated were in the vicinity of the camp and Newbridge every summer. His efforts succeeded to the extent that a lady was appointed to commence missionary work in Newbridge, and while there is no evidence of the success of her efforts, the problem of the fallen women remained unresolved.

A more enduring evangelical undertaking of John La Touche was the introduction of the Baptists to his locality about 1870. Outside the walls of Harristown he built a church, manse and school, all of which continue in their good work.

La Touche had a great love of his domain (almost 3,000 acres). This he showed one summer when holidaying in Lisdoonvarna. The location of the hotel he disliked, commenting, 'they might as well have built a monster hotel on Harristown Common as here.' He considered the scenery on Narraghmore Bog to be far more beautiful! He also had a romantic notion of the history of his estate, and he explained that the finding of a quantity of human bones in the *Relagheen Field* was evidence of an ancient battle between the Danes and the Swedes, but he could never remember where he had read the story! His wife commented that 'he never reads anything,' and she went to the National Museum in

*John La Touche, MFH of the Kildare Hunt*
*1841-1846*

Dublin to see the box of bones from the site. Dr Scharff at the museum asked her to bring a whole skull from the field, and when she told him that every one found was broken, he said, 'That was to be expected in an Irish battle!'

Another memorable happening recorded by Mrs La Touche was the great twenty-four hour down-pour in September 1883, when the cows drowned, haycocks and carts were carried away and the fields and gardens flooded: 'The river was a great broad sheet of brown and silver, calm at the sides, but all one terrible rush and swirl in the middle. No foam and no noise, but a frightful display of force and speed.' But there were more pleasant times, such as visits to officer friends on the Curragh, or outings to the Purcells at Narraghmore.

By the summer of 1885 the new railway line from Sallins to Baltinglass had been made through the Harristown property, with a convenient halt nearby. The construction of the line brought great joy to Mrs La Touche when she walked there: 'All the cuttings, embankments and stony heaps, are one sea of fire with scarlet poppies, making lines and lakes and mountains of flaming light as far as one can see along the line, and in broken heaps and masses, and scarlet spray beside it. Here and there, where the scarlet mass was less dense, a sort of gorgeous Eastern embroidery effect, from tall hawkweed and big daises rising through the poppies, and among them now and then a few tufts of grey poppies. I never saw or dreamt of such a revel of colour.'

In 1891 the La Touche mansion was accidentally damaged by fire (it was rebuilt, but lowered by a floor), and John moved his family to a cottage near the Baptist church. His wife commented: 'I get a good deal of entertainment, living next door to the Brannoxtown Baptist Chapel. They had a service last night, and no less than seventy people attended! Two carloads of soldiers came from the Curragh. As we sat at dinner I saw all the arrivals, and heard the opening hymn *Onwards Christian Soldiers* taken so fearfully slowly that one felt the Christian soldiers did not mean to hurry themselves, and evidently wished to remain non-combatants.'

The lady's philosophical outlook impressed one of her friends, who commented:

'I was much struck by her wisdom and calmness at the destruction of the Harristown fire, and so many beautiful works of art. No doubt she never quite took root there or indeed in the county. She felt herself 'living in *Boeotia*,' and perhaps not capable of loving house, furniture and chattels quite as ordinary folk.'

When Mrs La Touche had met the poet John Ruskin in London in 1858 she had invited him to advise on the education of their children, and a few years later he came to stay at Harristown. Though thirty years older than the youngest daughter, nine year old Rose, he became deeply attached to his 'mousepet in Ireland who nibbles me to the very sick-death with weariness to see her.' When she was seventeen he sought to marry her, but the family did not see him as a suitable husband. Apart from his age and the fact that his own marriage had been annulled, his philosophy was unacceptable. The pair parted, and seldom saw each other again. Rose died in 1875 at the age of twenty-six. Her elder sister, Emily, had also died at the same age, but their only brother Percy lived to inherit Harristown in 1904.

It was fortunate that Mrs La Touche was of a philosophical nature. She overcame the early deaths of her daughters, the religious fervour of her husband, and the pre-occupation of her neighbours with hunting, racing and gambling, by founding a Society of Souls, which she called *Althaeamen*, recalling the tragic classical *Althaea*. She, with Lady Drogheda of Moore Abbey, Lady Cloncurry of Lyons, and other like-minded ladies, adopted names from the classics, such as Stella, Lesbia and Althea, a conceit much scorned by their more mundane neighbours.

Maria La Touche wrote verse and sketched, and sometimes she expressed her views in the newspapers. In 1866 she sent a letter to the *Pall Mall Gazette* protesting against foxhunting, and she wrote a long poem on the subject for her friend Mr Mitchell of Ballynure, whom she regarded as 'the only philosopher in County Kildare.' She did not approve of the country house style of entertaining, asking 'why should social pleasure involve so much labour and anxiety, and expense? There was nothing spontaneous or impromptu about it, and very often when the main guest kept the party waiting, it put everyone else in bad humour. The practice of arranging partners at the table means than one could be bored for hours.' 'If one must entertain,' she suggested, 'a round table should be used, decorated with season flowers, and there should be few courses of the good food normally eaten, with wine, if there must be. There should be plenty of free talk,' that she believed, 'would constitute a party for rational beings.'

*Rose La Touche*

The Dublin Horse Show she found of less interest than Professor Barrett's lecture on Light, which she attended at the R.D.S. But she did believe in supporting local charity, and for a time was treasurer of the Kilcullen Dorcas Society, which was devoted to the care of the poor and the sick. While she cast a critical eye on all religions, she did commend the Catholics, being influenced, she thought, by 'the spirits of my grandmother and of my RC god-father.'

One day the local parson, Canon Somerville-Large, asked her to sign a petition requesting the Queen that convents should be inspected, she refused, saying 'I am sure the inspection would be considered a great insult by the conventual authorities, including their bishops. There are no doubt abuses, and perhaps cases of ill treatment, but so are there in households and families. We do not have nurseries and school rooms invaded and inspected because Mrs Montague killed her child...' Nevertheless, as was the practice in most big houses, the minimum of Roman Catholics was employed, and in 1901 there was but one amongst the six domestics in the house.

From the Shelbourne Hotel in Dublin in the spring of 1903 Mrs La Touche regretted that soon she must leave there, as 'it will be full of Punchestown, and then for that idiotic motor-race. All Ireland is inspired with wild frenzy for making money. A farmer in Kildare is asking for £20 for allowing people to encamp in a field, the annual rental of which is 10 shillings.'

She was referring to the first motor-race, named after James Gordon-Bennet, owner of the *New York Herald,* to be held in Ireland. It was to pass through Kilcullen, and on the eve of the big day Mrs La Touche with a companion went to Primrose Hill to watch the activity. This was her opinion: 'Lots of motors flashed past us, mostly tourists, flying in both directions. One stopped near us; the horrid thing was thirsty and too hot, or something. Clouds of dust are all that one could see, the solid monsters in their flight are only visible for one second. The whole thing so frightfully dangerous that it ought never to be allowed.'

John La Touche died in his ninety-first year in 1904, and his widow moved from Harristown to Dublin. It was said of him that 'he inherited even more than one man's share of the narrow evangelistic views held by his Trench relatives, and saw his way in later life to leave the Church of Ireland, but his interest in the antiquities of Kildare was not great. Not so Mrs La Touche, who combined a deep love of Ireland, its institutions and antiquities, with a keen interest in all that could promote culture. She looked on

*Harristown House*

the *Archaeological Society* of Kildare as a means to make the country less *Boeotian* (dull) if possible.' In an Obituary in *The Kildare Observer* it was recalled that 'when in the prime of life he had many Liberal leanings, and was in sympathy with the proposals of Land Reform...... but recently he refused to entertain any proposals for the sale of his property under the Land Purchase Act, and traversed the statement that the Irish landlords, as a body, were willing to sell. His funeral to the family vault, close to the main entrance to Harristown demesne, was of a private character, only relatives and immediate neighbours were present. The procession through the demesne was headed by the employees, who in turn assisted to take the remains, which were laid on a funeral car with pneumatic wheels, to the vault.'

That John's heir, Robert Percy O'Connor La Touche, was an eccentric but popular character is evident from this description of him from Lady Fingall: 'Percy could have done almost anything he chose to do. He had a brilliant brain, but he just amused himself and others. He was such an asset to a party and such a good sportsman, riding well and shooting well, that he could have lived forever in other people's houses. He was very poor, and he was untidy and careless in dress, and his nails were often unkempt. I used to say that he washed one ear twice and forgot the other. But no one minded these things. He helped to run Punchestown very efficiently, and otherwise he just shot and hunted.'

It was at Punchestown in 1904 that King Edward VII, when in a jovial mood, emphasised his remarks by inadvertently bringing his walking stick down on La Touche's shoulders: 'Whereupon, La Touche turned to His Majesty and said in rather a rueful manner 'Sir, I don't know whether you've knighted me or broken my collar bone'.'

Another story about him gave rise to the saying 'kiss me here, as Sir Percy said to the apple-woman.' It arose from a bet made by fellow members of the nobility at Punchestown. One of these gentlemen told a hawker that he would give her a sovereign if she went across and gave Sir Percy a kiss. The bould Percy, who must have had a sense of humour, overheard, and extending his cheek, in the loud ringing voice of the gentry of the time, invited her to '*kiss me here*'.

Robert Percy O'Connor La Touche, the last of the family to occupy Harristown, had married in 1870 Lady Annette-Louisa, a daughter of John Henry Scott, 3rd Earl of Clonmell of Bishopscourt, Straffan, and his wife Anne de Burgh, daughter of General Sir

*Four Generations of the La Touche family in 1894 – John and Maria La Touche with their son Percy, grand-daughter and great-grandson*

Ulysses de Burgh 2nd Lord Downes, of Bert, Athy. An elder daughter of the Clonmells had married Capt. George Fitzclarence RN, and their four sons joined the colours. One of them, Brig. Gen. Charles Fitzclarence, was awarded a V.C. for service in Africa.

La Touche was a steward of the Turf Club, a member of the Kildare Hunt Club, and of the Irish National Hunt Steeplechase Committee, and Manager of Punchestown from 1892 until his death in 1921. His association with Punchestown is marked with a Memorial Cup, awarded to the winner of a steeplechase over four and a quarter miles.

Percy La Touche left this recollection of Easter 1916. With a neighbour, and 'taking revolvers with them, just in case,' they drove into Dublin on Tuesday, 2 May. He saw that 'the streets were full of troops, armoured cars, ambulances and machine guns,' and wondered when racing might be able to start up again!

As the once celebrated Eustace family had vanished from Harristown, so did that of La Touche. A story told in the locality was that, early in the nineteenth century, Mr La Touche met a very poor man named Eustace who lived locally and he offered him help. Eustace refused the offer, saying, 'that his family was more used to the giving of alms than to accepting them!'

Though Harristown was sold in 1925, and again some years later, the house and the estate remain in good condition. Percy and Lady Annette La Touche are remembered in the beautiful memorial window, commissioned in 1921 from Harry Clarke by Canon Hannay (the writer George A. Bermingham), for the church of St Patrick at Carnalway, close to the gates of the La Touche estate at Harristown. The very suitable subject of the window is St Hubert, patron saint of hunters. There is now no inscription on the mausoleum outside the churchyard wall where the unhappy Rose La Touche was interred in 1875.

Harristown remains a family home and, on specified days, it is open to the public.

## Scotts of Bishopscourt

Sir Jonah Barrington, an impecunious lawyer of minor gentry background from near Abbeyleix, in 1827 commented critically on many of his contemporaries in his book *Personal Sketches of His Own Times*. Of the first Lord Clonmell, who was attorney general from 1777, he wrote: 'Mr Scott never omitted one favourable opportunity of serving himself. His skill was unrivalled and his success proverbial. He was full of anecdotes, though not the most refined: these in private society he not only told but acted; and when he perceived that he made a very good exhibition, he immediately withdrew, that he might leave the most lively impressions of his pleasantry behind him.' His connection with this county came with his marriage to Margaret Lawless, who was the only sister of the 1st Lord Cloncurry. Clonmell was popularly known as 'Copperfaced Jack', and he was notorious for his predilection to duelling, having himself fought four. As Attorney General he defended the practice: 'There are cases where it may be, and when it is prudent for a man to fight a duel, cases in which the law does not afford him redress, cases of persevering malignity, cases of injured honour, cases of wounded spirit, and a wounded spirit who can bear? In cases of this complexion the courts will never interfere with its discretionary authority against a man.'

Appropriately, it was near Bishopscourt that in 1815 Daniel O'Connell fought his duel with John D'Esterre, who died the next day from his wounds.

The Fenian Michael Davitt had little regard for Clonmell: 'The notorious Earl of Clonmell, one of the unscrupulous legal instruments of the landlord garrison. He died before the Act of Union became law, but his title was earned in like manner to that of the ancestors of the present Irish nobility.'

In 1838 John Henry Scott, the third Earl of Clonmell, joined the ranks of the county gentry when on his marriage he purchased Bishopscourt, Straffan, with its 1,958 acres. The fine classical house there had been built by Rt. Hon. John Ponsonby, Speaker of the Irish House of Commons in the mid eighteenth century. Of his son, William Brabazon Ponsonby, it was said 'that he kept the best hunting establishment in Ireland at Bishopscourt, where he lived in the most hospitable and princely style.' He took his pack to hunt in County Carlow in 1792 and the *Sporting Magazine* reported that: 'Although the turnout of the Bishopscourt Hunt itself was not, from the sombre uniform of its members, as flashing and as striking to some eyes who like to dwell on some hundred to hundred and fifty cavaliers decked in scarlet and gold, yet to my eye, which was caught more by the aristocratic Master himself than the coat he had on, the splendid and numerous pack of well-bred, well-matched English dogs, the blue coat and velvet cape lined with buff, the broad-striped blue and buff waistcoat, yellow buckskins, in fact the dress of the Fox Club, with a large yellow button in which was embossed a fox's pate, around which, in large legible characters *Bishopscourt Hunt,* appeared quite as aristocratic as anyone need wish.'

Frederick Ponsonby was a bachelor and the last of the family to live at Bishopscourt. He too was a great sportsman, and he presented the *Ponsonby Bowl* to be run for at the Kildare Hunt races. When he died in 1849 his funeral was met by the people at Rathcoole, the coffin taken from the hearse and carried to Oughterard Hill, where he was buried. Not too far distant from Oughterard the family is remembered in the *Ponsonby Bridge,* over the Grand Canal.

The 3rd Earl of Clonmell, successor of the Ponsonbys at Bishop's Court, was also a keen supporter of the Kildare Hunt Club, and Master of Fox Hounds from 1854-57. His Mastership was immortalised when Michael Angelo Hayes painted his portrait, surrounded by members of the hunt in front of Bishopscourt. He was also amongst those worthies who entertained in their own tents during the annual Punchestown Meeting.

The Earl was known for his strange sense of humour, an example of which was the story that one day as he was driving a nervous friend along the tow path of the Grand Canal his lordship remarked 'What, never been in the canal?' immediately driving down the bank and turning himself, his friend, and the whole machine into the water. Another

*3rd Earl of Clonmell in 1862*

story, told by Mark Bence Jones, was that at a reception in Dublin Castle the Earl, having had too many drinks, 'sat down heavily on the brocaded lap of a portly dowager, which in his condition he mistook for an armchair.'

Clonmell died at the age of forty-nine in 1866. He was remembered as a kind and considerate landlord who, during the Famine, said to his agent 'I am fond of hunting, but I will part with hunters, hounds and servants rather than let my tenants want.' Another tribute came from the historian Bernard Fitzpatrick: 'Old habitués of Punchestown will remember Lord Clonmell as, with long thong whip in hand, dressed in the scarlet uniform of the Kildare Hunt Club, and mounted on his favourite white horse, he cantered up and down the rails, cheerily rating the rustics with whom, as with those of his own rank, he was an especial favourite.'

His son, the 4th Earl, inherited his father's mischievous humour, and he was celebrated for the great parties which he gave during Punchestown. As Mark Bence-Jones has commented 'he was inclined to do his guests and also himself rather too well; there are many stories told of his exploits when in his cups, such as when Queen Victoria smiled graciously on him at a garden party and he rushed over to her, shook her warmly by the hand and assured her that he knew her face but could not for the moment remember her name.'

## Cloncurrys and Blackers

After an occupancy of five hundred years the Aylmer family in 1796 sold their estate at Lyons, near Celbridge, to the first Lord Cloncurry. Nicholas Lawless, who was from a Dublin family of wealthy wool merchants and drapers; as a Catholic he was sent to Rouen to be educated, and for a time he settled there. In 1767 he came home to join the family business, and one of his first acts was to conform to the Established Church. As it was remarked later 'if he had not (conformed) it is not very probable he would ever have become Lord Baron Cloncurry.' Created a baronet in 1782, he acquired a peerage seven years later.

Michael Davitt, the nationalist and labour leader writing in 1904, believed that Cloncurry's title 'was purchased for money, the cash being expended in the cause of the Union. Curran, the famous advocate and wit, alluding to this and similar transactions, said: 'The sale of peerages is as notorious as the sale of cart-horses in the Castle Yard; the publicity the same, the terms not any different, the horses not warranted sound, the other animals warranted rotten.' Lawless had turned Protestant in order to buy landed property, and he then bought himself a peerage by helping to sell the Parliament of his country.'

As a baronet Cloncurry had continued to attend country fairs 'with his three cornered hat and courtly attire, standing in the middle of a knot of country clowns, while he endeavoured to conclude a hard-fought bargain for the purchase of a half-dozen load of wool packs.' Intent on establishing himself as a gentleman, Cloncurry brought the bones of his ancestors from Crumlin in Dublin for reburial at Lyons, in the old Aylmer graveyard, an arrangement which was to cause anguish to the Aylmer family. He engaged an architect named Grace to build a suitable house, which included its own private station on the Grand Canal, of which company he was a director. When he died in 1799 he was buried at Lyons.

Lord Cloncurry's eldest daughter, Mary, had married Thomas Whalley of Whalley Abbey, County Wicklow. He was the eccentric *Buck* or *Jerusalem Whalley* who, for a wager made during dinner one evening at Leinster House, home of William Robert, 2nd duke of Leinster, had succeeded in travelling to Jerusalem, playing hand-ball against the city walls, and returning home within a year. The marriage took place in 1800, when the bride's brother, Valentine, was an untried prisoner in the Tower of London. But the union lasted less than a year. Whalley died at thirty-four years of age, it was rumoured from a stab-wound inflicted by a jealous woman, and his widow was left to care for his three 'natural' children.

His Lordship's only sister, Margaret Lawless, had married John Scott, Lord Clonmell, and as his Countess she merited mention in the *Memoirs* of Mrs Leeson, the celebrated Dublin *Madame* of that period. Mrs Leeson makes frequent reference to her keeper and lover Buck Lawless, who was Lady Clonmell's brother. On one occasion she recalled that 'Mr Lawless, a near relation of the Countess of Clonmell, thinking to give me a pleasurable jaunt, proposed that we should go to the Curragh races. There, having feasted our eyes with all that was to be seen, we went to Burchell's at the *Nineteen-Mile- House,* for some refreshments,' but they then had difficulty in finding accommodation, and the excursion did not end happily.

Lord Cloncurry's only son, Valentine-Browne Lawless, 2nd Baron, following education on the continent, returned to Kildare in 1795. A friend of Lord Edward FitzGerald, Lawless joined the United Irishmen, and he accompanied FitzGerald to the trials of accused men to show that their commitment was to the rank and file. In November 1796 Lord Edward had signed an agreement with Lawless's mother, Lady Cloncurry, which mortgaged his Kilrush estate to her for two years and fifteen hundred pounds, perhaps as Stella Tillyard surmises in her book *Citizen Lord,* to purchase weapons for the United Irishmen. A couple of years later Valentine published an anti-Union pamphlet and his father, to avoid trouble, sent him to study in London, but there he was apprehended and incarcerated in the Tower, during which time he succeeded to the title.

On his release from prison, Cloncurry travelled to Rome where he numbered amongst his friends the president of the Irish College. In that ancient city 'he derived much recreation from excavating among the Baths of Titus and elsewhere in the hope of finding some old articles of *virtu.*' His eventual collection he shipped back to Lyons, including one consignment which was lost when the *Aid* was wrecked in Killiney Bay. That some of his treasures reached home was evident when he presented the white conch-shaped marble holy water font, which Pope Pius VII had given him, to the chapel at Ardclough. It is now at Lyons.

By the time Cloncurry returned home he was thirty years of age, and married to the teen-age daughter of Major General George Morgan. They had two infants, Valentine-Anne who died unmarried in 1825, and Mary Margaret, who, in time, would marry the Baron de Robeck of Naas. Happily settled at Lyons, the young lord engaged Sir Richard Morrison to improve the house and grounds. Using some of the antique columns brought from Italy, he added a pedimented portico and, as he was to do later at Carton, Morrison straightened the colonnades. The interior of Lyons was embellished in the classical mode; a frieze of ox heads, pillars, and romantic Irish frescos by Gabrielli, the Italian painter who had accompanied the Cloncurrys home from Italy. A greater than life-size bust of *Hibernia and Cloncurry,* by John Hogan, originally at Lyons, is now in the National Gallery. A magnificent formal garden linked the house to a large artificial lake beneath the Hill of Lyons.

But life was not all bliss. Within a few years of his marriage there was gossip that his old school friend, Sir John Bennet Piers, a widower from County Westmeath to whom Cloncurry had loaned money, made a wager that he could wreck the happy home. Piers was later described somewhat ambiguously as being both 'of good character and having spent four years in the army,' and as 'a gambler, duellist, and spendthrift!'

By persistent effort he alienated Lady Cloncurry's affections to such an extent that a duel was fought between Cloncurry and Piers. On that same day Cloncurry ordered Lady Cloncurry's maid to sleep in future with her Ladyship, declaring that he 'would sleep with her no more;' and within a short time she had left the house for good.

On the 19 February 1807 before a jury at the King's Bench, the Plaintiff, The Right Honourable Valentine-Browne Lawless, Lord Baron Cloncurry, charged Sir John Bennet Piers, Bart, Defendant, 'of a plea of trespass with force and arms, for that the said Sir John Bennet Piers on the 21st day of April 1806, at College-green, in the county of the city of Dublin, with force and arms, on Eliza Georgiana, then and yet the wife of the said Lord Baron Cloncurry, did make an assault, and did then and there ravish, embrace, debauch, lie with, and carnally know, by means whereof the said Lord Cloncurry lost, and was deprived of the comfort, society, love and affection of his said wife.' Lady Cloncurry's maid gave evidence that one day she found her mistress 'sitting on the pier table, and Sir John Pier's chair was convenient; she was in a very delicate state, and her kerchief much discomposed, and upon my coming in, Sir John Piers jumped suddenly behind a stuffed-back chair, seemingly to hide the discomposure of his dress. He then spoke in a language that I did not understand, and Lady Cloncurry ordered me to leave the room.' Being further questioned on the state of her ladyship's dress, the maid revealed 'It was indelicate, her habit shirt was tore open, her breasts quite bare, and her face was violently red.'

In the report of the trial it was noted 'that the adulterous connexion has been fruitful, within a short time Lady Cloncurry has been delivered of a son, and there is little doubt of this child being the spurious offspring of her guilt. This infant becomes entitled to some of Lord Cloncurry's property, and in the course of human events, may be the inheritor of his estates. Every feeling of disgust and horror, of which the human heart is capable, must be excited in the breast of Lord Cloncurry, when he thinks upon this atrocious aggravation of his miseries.'

But in evidence at the Parliamentary Divorce hearings in 1811 Lord Cloncurry explained that he had allowed Lady Cloncurry to remain in the house for a short time as 'she was an Englishwoman, that she had no place where she could get protection in Ireland, and that the person who had seduced her was in the neighbourhood. I wrote to her father within half an hour of the time I received the information of her criminality; and by the advice of her friends, I allowed her to remain, her own maid constantly sleeping with her.' The case concluded and the marriage was dissolved by Act of Parliament, with a judgement of £20,000 damages, and 6d costs against the adulterer, Sir John Piers, Bart. The case was immortalised in a cartoon entitled *Crim. Con.* which depicts the guilty couple being sketched by Gabrielli from his platform, and captioned '*A Sketch taken from Life by Seignoir Gabrielli. Valued by 12 Connoisseurs at Twenty Thousand pounds!*' So interesting was the trial, two reports were published by rival publishers, and their sale was described as 'immense'. The English Poet Laureate Sir John Betjeman wrote a poem on the subject, of which this is a fragment:

> Oh, gay lapped the waves on the shores of Lough Ennell
> ( … )
> And a boatload of beauty darts over the tide,
> The Baron Cloncurry and also his bride.
> ( … )
> But why has the Lady Cloncurry such fears?
> Oh, one of the guests will be Baronet Piers.

( ... )

The harness is off with a jingle of steel,

The grey in the grass crops an emerald meal,

Sir John saunters up with a smile and a bow

And the Lady Cloncurry is next to him now.

Her eyes on the landscape, she don't seem to hear,

The passing remarks he designs for her ear,

For smooth as a phantom and proud as a stork

The Lady Cloncurry continues her walk.

Both parties soon remarried, Lady Cloncurry to a clergyman, but she pined for her children who had remained with Lord Cloncurry. In the papers of the confidential agent of Cloncurry, Thomas Ryan, J.P. of Ballinakill, quoted by William John Fitzpatrick in his book published in 1855 'The Life, Times, and Contemporaries of Lord Cloncurry', her ladyship's distress is revealed in the correspondence he received from her for many years afterwards. 'Nothing can be more painfully interesting than this correspondence. Our eyes suffused with tears as we read it. It breathes the holiest sentiments from the first to the last, fond inquiries after the health of her children, their juvenile progress in knowledge and religion; whether they ever speak of their poor, poor mother; anxious aspirations that they may be good and happy.' In more than one letter, Lady Cloncurry beseeches Mr Ryan 'to endeavour to steal for her a lock of Valentine's and Mary's hair, in order that she may place it next her heart, and sigh and cry over it.'

Cloncurry married the widow of Hon. Joseph Leeson of Russborough, and mother of the 4th Earl of Milltown. Her children with Cloncurry, included Edward 3rd Baron Cloncurry, and Cecil John, a Member of Parliament, who in time married the widow of John William Digby of Landenstown. The Digby family was settled here since the early eighteenth century, sometimes filling the offices of high sheriff and members of parliament. Simon Digby was an officer of the Volunteer Clane Rangers on its formation in 1779, and he is mentioned in the ballad of that name: *Then Digby, tho' invited to Geashill's large Corps, Joins His Grace* (the Duke of Leinster) *sword in hand, and to Clane he rides o'er.* The avenue of their mid-eighteenth century Landenstown house was severed by the making of the Grand Canal, but the bridge at the entrance gates preserves the Digby name.

Valentine Lawless took an active part in the life of the county; he was a magistrate, and he inaugurated a system of petty-sessions which was later adopted nationally. A director of the Grand Canal County, he was also a founder member of the *County Kildare Farming Society,* and in the famine year of 1847 he employed 'upwards of seventy labourers' at Lyons. A supporter of the Roman Catholics, and a benefactor of the college at Mount St Joseph, Clondalkin, he laid the foundation stone of the chapel there.

That Cloncurry enjoyed visiting his neighbours is apparent from his *Personal Reminiscences,* published in 1849. He commented that 'there was hardly a great house where some frolicsome younger brother or elderly uncle could not be found, whom no one would have dreamed of trusting with any duty more important than that of mixing punch or the purveying of game for the family table.'

But he himself was also commented on, by Lady Milltown and her friend Mrs Elizabeth Smith of Baltyboys. The latter confided in her diary: The vain old man has made an amusing book though probably not a very veracious one and he has taken a good many liberties with names and family histories. His genealogy is incorrect, he does not belong to the respectable Lawlesses he claims descent from; his grandfather was nobody knows who, his father a wool comber and got on by talents, chance and industry. I sent her (Lady Milltown) the book yesterday as they can't afford to buy it, and it was not sent to them. Lady Milltown is very angry at figuring in it; Edward Lawless (his son and heir) very much annoyed and several persons who consider themselves aggrieved by his representations have forced him to make apologies in the newspapers. He is well used to that for many of his own letters in these Memoirs are in the same strain for the same cause, first a bluster, then a rebuke, and next regrets. Edward, the 3rd Baron Cloncurry, and his wife Elizabeth Kirwan, of Castle Hackett, County Galway, had five sons and four daughters. But the family was a tragic one, with the baron and two of his daughters dying by suicide.

The best known member of that family was the Hon. Emily Lawless who wrote many patriotic novels and a biography of Maria Edgeworth. She once mused: 'We are children of our environment, the good no less than the bad, products of that particular group of habits, customs, traditions, ways of looking at things, standards of right and wrong, which chance has presented to our still growing and expanding consciousness.' Her book of verse *With the Wild Geese* was very successful, and the lines from *After Aughrim* were familiar to countless school children:

> She said, God knows they owe me nought.
>  I tossed them to the foaming sea,
>  I tossed them to the howling waste,
>  Yet still their love comes home to me.

Emily's brother Valentine, the 4th Lord Cloncurry, according to Mark Bence-Jones, 'was noted for his mauve beard, which had been turned that colour by some patent restorative; hostesses would complain that when he stayed in their houses he left mauve stains on the bed sheets.' With the death in 1929 of his brother, Frederick 5th Baron Cloncurry, who was Governor of the National Gallery, the title became extinct, and almost forty years ago the Lyons estate was sold following the death of the last Miss Lawless.

Having passed through a number of owners, the house and gardens of the 600-acre walled demesne are now faithfully restored by Dr Tony Ryan, but the splendid *Hibernia with the bust of Valentine Lawless* by John Hogan (1841) which was in the house, is now displayed in the National Gallery, Dublin.

Mary, the youngest of Emily Lawless' three sisters, was married in 1877 to William Blacker of Castlemartin, Kilcullen, which estate had been purchased in 1854. The house had been built above and around a Eustace castle by a Dublin banker about 1720, and in 1798 it had served as headquarters for General Dundas. It is situated above the river Liffey in a magnificently wooded estate of 948 acres (in 1908), and close-by, a ruined fifteenth century church and an Eustace effigy.

The demise of the Blacker family was tragic. The widowed Sheila Blacker, having lost her eldest son in the Second World War, lived alone in the mansion in straightened circumstances. Her other son, Percy, and his wife Anna Flaherty from the Aran Islands, lived close-by at Kinneagh. Anna Blacker died in 1966 and Sheila Blacker in the following year. Soon after his mother's death Percy was returning from Dublin, where he had been consulting his solicitor, when he was killed by a car while hitching a lift at the Red Cow Inn, Clondalkin. Castlemartin was inherited by the earl of Gowrie, who sold it to Sir Anthony O'Reilly about two decades ago. He had the ruined medieval church restored for worship; and as the Lawless family had done at Lyons two hundred years earlier, O'Reilly did at Castlemartin. He has converted the graveyard to family use by exhuming the remains of his father in Dublin and reentering them at Castlemartin.

*Lord Cloncurry*

## Cooke-Trench of Millicent

In the first volume of the *Journal of the County Kildare Archaeological Society*, published in the last decade of the nineteenth century, Thomas Cooke-Trench, a founding-member of the Society, contributed a note on the Ashe family of Moone, to which he was related. He referred to a seventeenth century family bible in which there was the entry: 'Abraham Swift and Martha Cooke were married on 24 June 1680.' Martha came from a family of merchants of wealth and position in the city of Dublin, having been frequently Sheriffs and Lord Mayors; Thomas Ashe had purchased the manor of Moone in 1703, which had been forfeited by Thomas and Maurice Eustace in the Rebellion of 1641. He had willed that his body 'should be interred in the most private manner by my executers, nine feet deep in the centre of the mount in the mountfield, being part of my estate of Moone.'

When Thomas Cooke-Trench, whose father Thomas Trench had been a lieutenant in the Royal Horse Artillery, died at Millicent, Sallins, in November 1902, 'at the ripe old age of seventy-three years,' he merited a long Obituary in *The Leinster Leader*. It noted that 'Thomas had resumed by patent the name and arms of Trench in conjunction with those of Cooke in 1858, and around that time he had also purchased the lands at Millicent. His wife was the eldest daughter of an English gentleman who was for many years MP for the University of Oxford.'

Cooke-Trench was a member of the Naas Board of Guardians for over forty years, a record also held by the Baron de Robeck and John La Touche. He was also a High Sheriff of the County and a member of the County Kildare Committee of Agriculture and Technical Instruction since its formation. He travelled throughout Europe, and to the Holy Land. His devotion to his family was evident in the fact that for over thirty years he recorded its history, a task which the writer of his obituary believed 'was of course of no real interest to anyone outside the connections of the family and the ranks of genealogists, but it may be cited as a proof of the great tenacity with which Cooke-Trench carried out any purpose to which he set his mind.'

## Wilson-Wright of Coolcarrigan

In 1908 Coolcarrigan, the Wilson estate near Timahoe, embraced 5,432 acres, a substantial enlargement from William Wilson's holding of 1,844 acres in 1853. The Wilson family had come to county Kildare from County Antrim. Robert Mackay Wilson of Coolcarrigan was a Justice of the Peace and High Sheriff in 1887, and his heir, Jane Georgina married in 1889 Prof. Sir Almroth Edward Wright, a celebrated pathologist. Their son adopted the surname Wilson-Wright. Sir Henry Wilson, former Chief of the Imperial Staff, who was murdered by the IRA in London in 1922, was a cousin of Jane Wilson Wright.

Inside the demesne at Coolcarrigan there is a small church, entered through a lych gate. It was built by the family in 1884, and the design is based on that of a ruined church at Clonmacnoise. It has been described as 'the most perfect example of the Celtic Revival in Ireland.' The stained glass windows by Catherine O'Brien were inspired by illustrations in the Book of Kells, and the scriptural texts on the walls were designed by Dr Douglas Hyde, first President of Ireland, who was a friend of the family.

## The Guinness Family

The Guinness family of Leixlip prospered in the liquor trade. Arthur Guinness, a brewer in Leixlip in 1756, was the son of a land agent and the founder of the Guinness empire, which, until very recent years, controlled the St James's Gate brewery in Dublin. Arthur died in 1803 and was buried at Oughterard. His very prosperous successors lived in Dublin and London, and gradually progressed into high society. In 1881 Edward Guinness, who was later ennobled as the 1st Earl of Iveagh, enlarged Farmleigh, an early nineteenth century house at Castleknock. It remained in the family until recent years when it was purchased by the State. It was not until after the Second World War that a branch of the Guinness family was again established in County Kildare.

Richard Guinness, a company director in England, purchased Lodge Park, the old Henry family house at Straffan. His son Robert now has a Steam Museum there which, with the gardens, is seasonally opened to the public. His daughter Shaunagh is married to Col. Anthony Aylmer of the Courtown, Kilcock family.

In the 1950s a son of Lord Moyne and Lady Mosley (née Diana Mitford), the Hon. Desmond Guinness, and his wife Princess Mariga von Urach, came to live in County Kildare, first at Carton, and then at Leixlip Castle. There in 1958 they founded the *Irish Georgian Society*, while they also restored and refurbished their medieval home.

A decade later the Guinness's purchased the endangered Castletown House at Celbridge, and made it the headquarters of the *Irish Georgian Society*, from whom it came into the care of *Dúchas* in 1995. There are now four Guinness households in the county, as the son and daughter of the Hon. Desmond & Mrs Guinness live respectively at Furness and at Pickering Forest. Pickering was formerly the home of the family of Sir George Brooke, 1st Br. Summerton.

Furness, which was built around 1740 for Richard Nevill, was purchased in 1897 by Wexford born Nicholas J. Synnott, who was a High Sheriff of the County Kildare, and Governor of the Bank of Ireland. His son, Maj. Pierce Synnott, served in the British army in North Africa and the Middle East during the Second World War; afterwards he returned to his old post at the Admiralty, and from which he retired as Under-Secretary.

Back at Furness he resumed his interest in *The County Kildare Archaeological Society*, and was elected president, and in the Irish Association of the Sovereign Military Order of Malta, of which he was chancellor until he died in 1983. He was succeeded by his only son, David, who in recent years sold Furness.

Above: *Leixlip Castle in 1861 from the Illustrated Dublin Journal*

Left: *Mrs Synnott and the standing stone in the rath at Furness in 1900*

# 9

# Behind the Walls

In the making and maintenance of the demesnes and mansions of the genteel class great numbers of men and women were employed and, generally speaking, the retainers of the gentry were materially better off than the landless masses that did not live within the estate boundaries. If the crimes of the bad landlords are remembered, the humanity and benevolence of others are often forgotten. When the injustices of the past, such as evictions or land seizures, are recalled it must be remembered that the perpetrators of such acts could, as easily, have been from Gaelic or Anglo-Norman Roman Catholic families, as from those of English Protestant descent. Very often the villains were 'strong' farmers or middlemen, just as those who exploited the food shortage of the famines included shopkeepers and *gombeen* men.

The imbalance of society in the early eighteenth century was described by historian Victoria Glendinning:

'All that the ladies and gentlemen from Dublin saw, as they drove to and from country houses through the depressed and depressing countryside, were bands of ragged men and women, eking out their wretched lives, with no employment and with swarms of children whom they could not support, living in lightless mud cabins, talking a barbaric, language, begging and stealing, apparently pig-ignorant and uninvolved.'

Mark Bence-Jones, a contemporary writer with a gentry background, commented on the Ascendancy:

'It is easy enough to say that if only they had farmed their lands more efficiently they would still be able to maintain their ancestral homes; but during the past century just as many well-farmed family estates have been sold up as neglected ones. It is again easy to say that if only they had not on the whole been so loyal to the Crown, and so determined to maintain the Union with Britain, they would have been able to play a more significant part in the life of the new independent Ireland; but while there were always some nationalists among the Ascendancy, their families are now just as much outside the mainstream of present-day Irish life as those with a Unionist tradition.'

Another offspring of the 'big house', the novelist Elizabeth Bowen, mused:

'Is it height, in this country of otherwise low buildings that got these Anglo-Irish houses their 'big' name? Or have they been called 'big' with a slight inflection, that of hostility, irony? One may call a man 'big' with just that inflection because he seems to think the hell of himself.'

Those sentiments were echoed by Brian Fallon, writing in the *Irish Times* a few years ago:

'Many or most of them (the gentry) ultimately came to terms with the new order, and in any case the Anglo-Irish land-owning caste was probably doomed historically. There was endemic land hunger to satisfy old social and economic grudges which ached, vicious class differences, yawning religious divides, the challenge of new, nativist class structures and social forces emerging; the constitutional means were simply not there to cope with this.'

More recently, writing in the same newspaper, Robert O'Byrne gave his opinion of the gentry:

'Many of our grandest houses were originally built with newly-minted money: Lyons by Lord Cloncurry, the son of a wealthy blanket manufacturer; Castletown by self-made William Conolly; and Russborough by the first Earl of Milltown, whose father, a precursor of the Guinness dynasty, had been a successful brewer....this remains true of to-day's Irish *nouveaux riches*. Castlemartin, Lyons.... classically designed country houses now owned by members of Ireland's new rich club; other than acting as clear statements of wealth, they serve little purpose, since such buildings can no longer be financially supported by the estates of which they were once the centrepiece.'

Indeed, Major John de Burgh of Oldtown recalled in 2000 that in his youth he often heard his father, when discussing new arrivals on the County scene, wondering if they could be considered gentry or not!

Of course the ordinary people, accustomed to the loud hunting-field English accents of the Anglo Irish, had their own opinions of them, and these were sometimes expressed in proverbs such: *Na bhi ag rith i ndiadh na huaisle*. (Do not be running after the gentry), and the admonition: *Na tabahir dod dhailtin coir nach cuibhe dho, Na comhluadar le huaslibh tire; Mura gcoinnir smachtaithe e is e 'chomead foriseal. Is meas le cothu na coilean mac tire.* (Child rearing: Keep him away from the company of gentry; give him only what befits a child. If you don't keep him strict within the bounds of decency he'll be harder to rear than the wolves of the wild.)

Then there was the old adage: *Gentry sent to market will not buy one bushel of corn* (The implication is that noble blood alone is of no material value).

Unsurprisingly, Brendan Behan had his own perception of the 'Class'. In his play *The Hostage* he offered a succinct definition of an Anglo-Irishman: 'A Protestant on a horse!' And another time he quipped: 'Compliments pass when the quality meet'.

A former Irish army officer, Major Patrick Colgan, who fought in the War of Independence, also had a caustic opinion of the Gentry. Recollecting that period, he wrote in 1949:

'Maynooth was and is a poor village; mainly it was poor because all the land was held by few. It was the happy hunting ground for the retired Colonels, Majors and Captains of the British Army. The few non-ex-military landed in the area were graziers who aped 'their betters'. Outside the Duke of Leinster's estate and St Patrick's College there was little or no employment. Everything was taken from the 'big house', except religion. The little I knew of the personnel in charge of Maynooth College at that time made me feel that their National outlook was no better than that of the 'big house' crowd.'

# Index